Windows 10:

2020 Beginners Guide to Unlock the True Potential of your Operating System 50 Things you need to know about Windows 10.

ISBN: 9798665716381

CONTENTS

Introduction

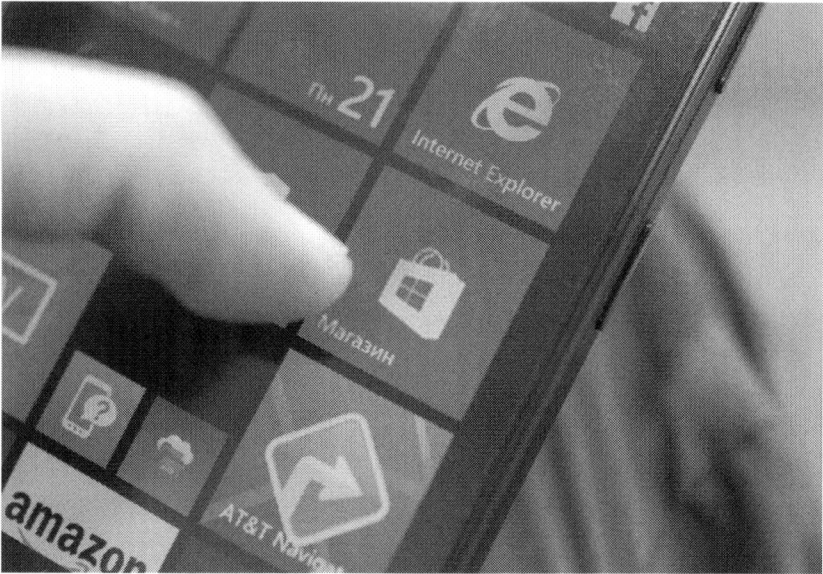

Windows 10 is the most popular operating system in the world. But what do you know about it?

In our book, we will give you the most necessary instructions for using this operating   system.

Chapter 1: Downloading and Installing Windows 10 on your Personal Computer

This chapter is for those who have not already installed Windows 10. If you already have an operating system installed, go to the next chapter.

If you actively use your personal computer and if you already have Windows 7 or Windows 8, you can upgrade to Windows 10 using the standard system update mechanism. You should just turn on the Windows Update service.

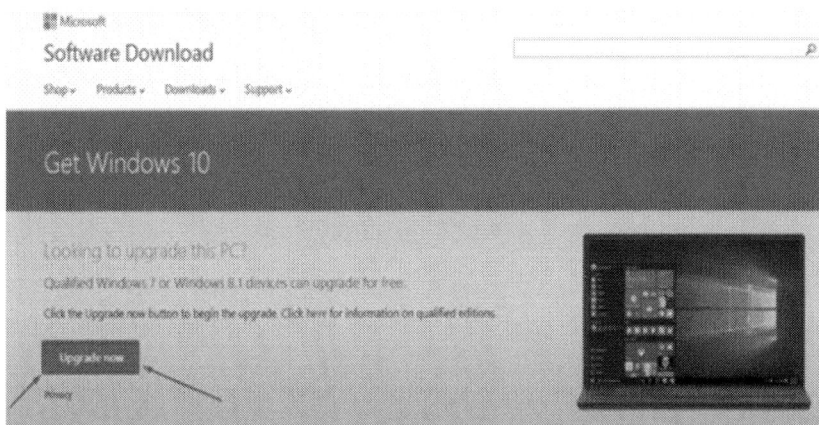

The Installation of Windows 10 will be needed only if you bought a new computer without an operating system and purchased the Windows 10

installation disc separately. Or if you needed a clean installation of Windows 10. Installing Windows 10 is almost the same as Windows 7, but there is one point.

Typically, licensed Windows 10 ships on a DVD. To install it, you just need to insert the disk into the drive and restart your personal computer.

If your computer is not equipped with a CD rom, you need to place the Windows 10 image on a flash drive and boot it from the flash drive and install Windows 10.

There are many ways to create a bootable flash drive.

1. Using the standard tool from

Microsoft - Windows 10 Installation Media Creation Tool, which can be downloaded at: https://www.microsoft.com/software-download/windows10

This process is very easy: you need to choose which edition you will install. Next, you just download and install it on your flash drive

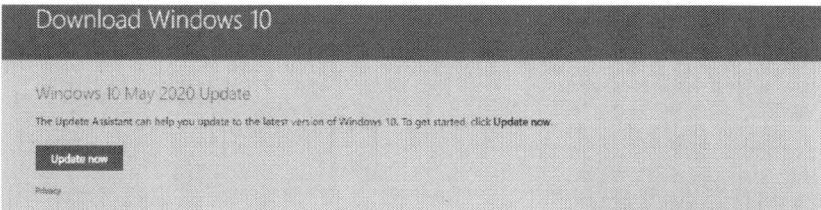

Step One: Launch Windows 10

Installation Media Creation Tool

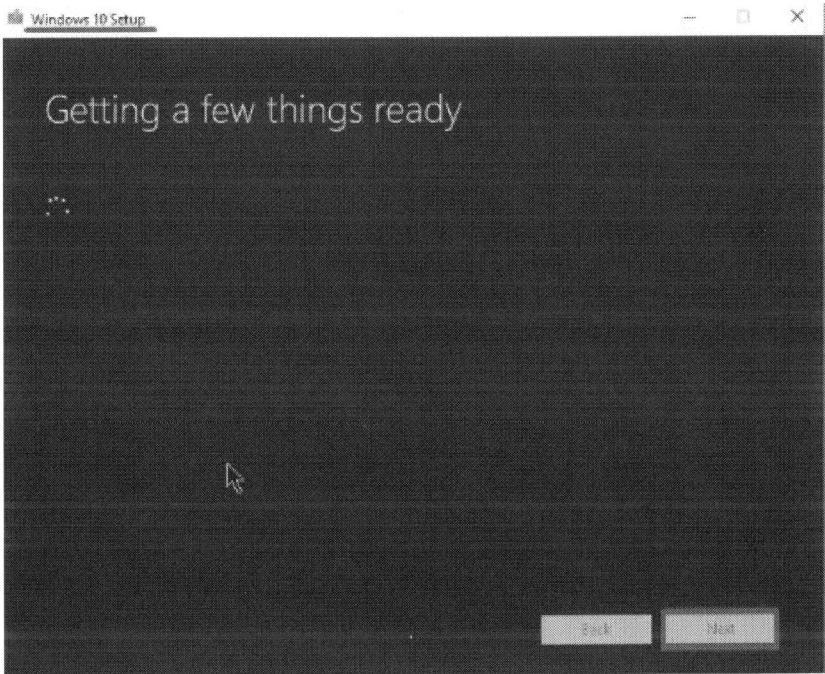

Step Two: Choose to create an installation media and press next.

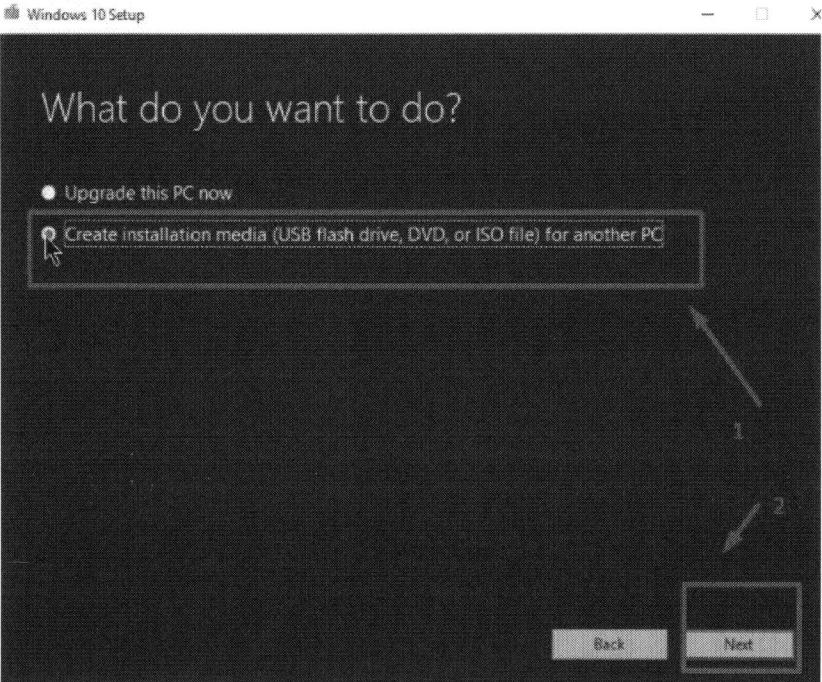

This is the only official way. If you already have an ISO image that you got somewhere (for example, you created it with the same program or created it yourself from the installation disk using the Nero program or similar), then you can use the Windows 7 USB / DVD Download Tool.

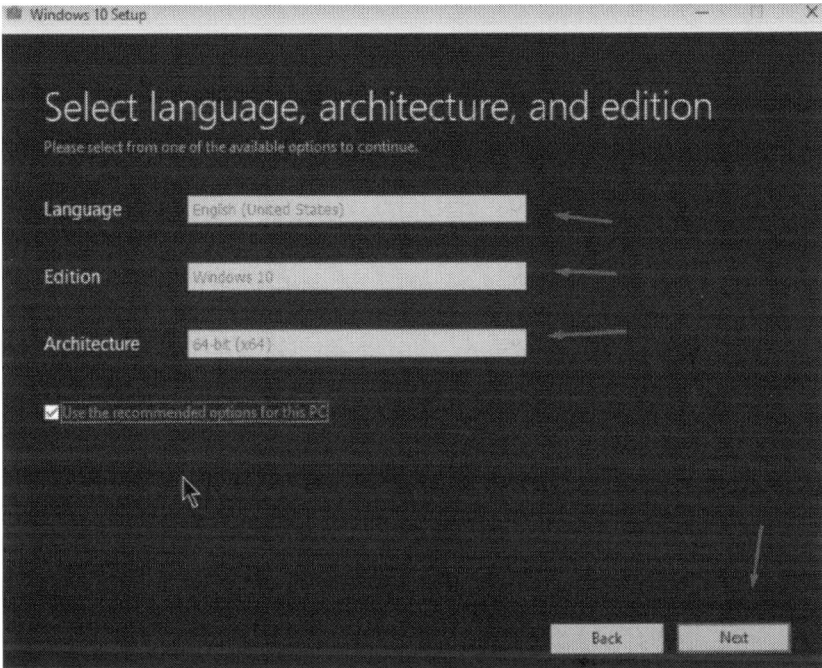

As in the picture above, you should choose the language, edition and architecture (32/64 bit). Next, you click Next.

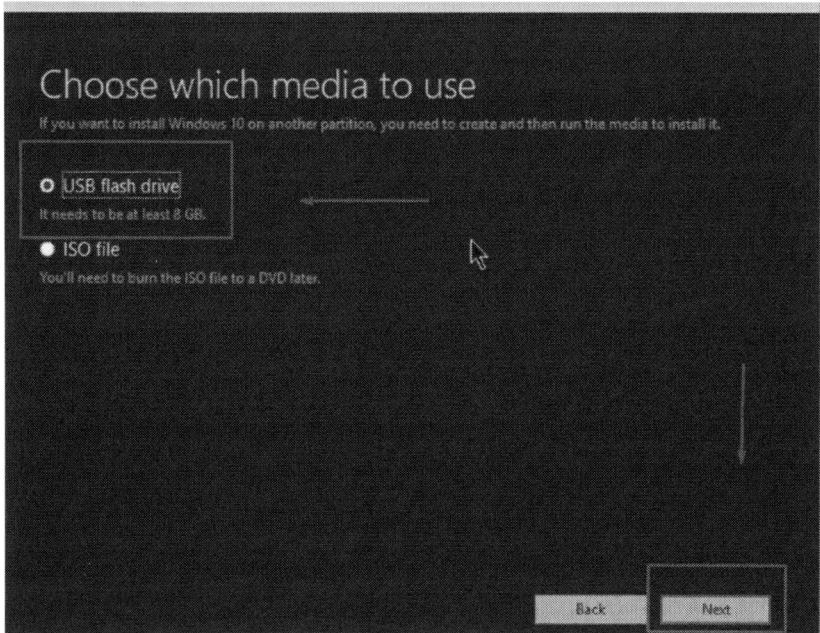

Then you should choose USB flash drive and click Next

Windows 10

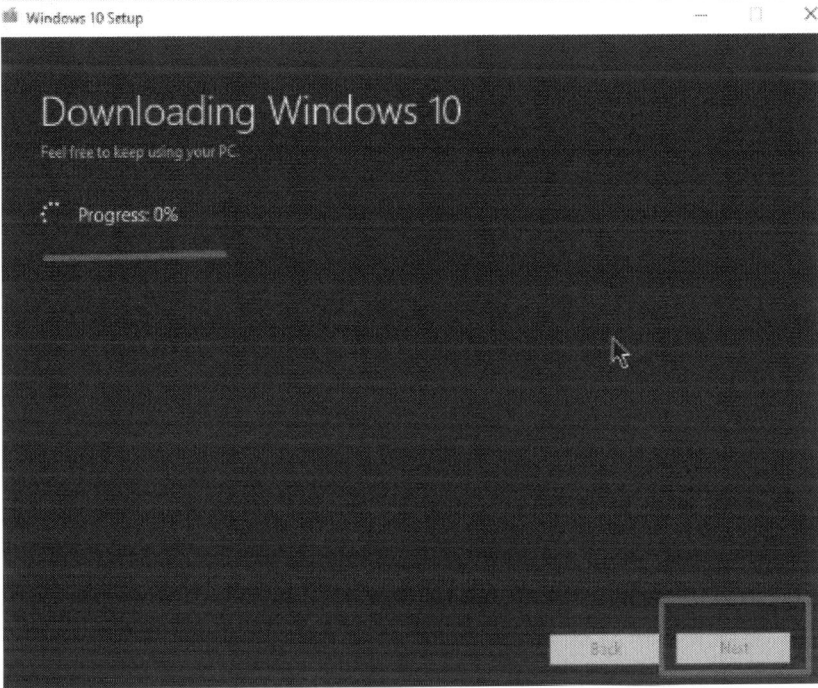

Windows 10 Setup

Downloading Windows 10

Feel free to keep using your PC.

Progress: 0%

Back   Next

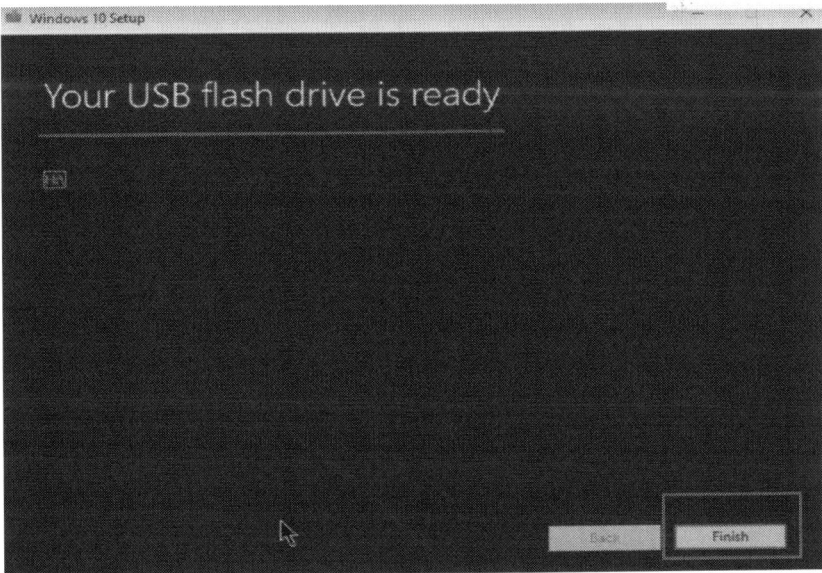

Windows 10 Setup

Your USB flash drive is ready

Back   Finish

Next, you click Finish to complete. Your installation disc is ready. After that, you insert your USB flash into the slot and restart the computer. If everything is set up correctly, then the automatic installation of Windows 10 begins.

You click install now and follow the instructions.

Installing Windows 10 on your Personal Computer

To get started, you need to go into the BIOS SETUP of your computer and select the boot from a DVD or flash drive (depending on the type of media from which you will install Windows). On desktop computers, the DEL key is usually used to enter the BIOS SETUP. On laptops, there may be other keys and even key combinations.

In order to enter the BIOS Setup Utility, you must press a certain keyboard key (sometimes you need to press a key combination) during the ICT procedure (ICT-initial computer testing, which is performed immediately after turning on the PC).

I note that the most common option for

entering the BIOS is to use the Delete key, the keys F1, F2 are used a little less often.

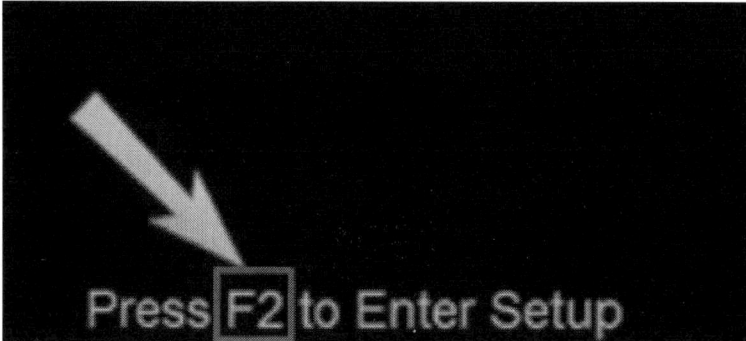

There are two ways to find out the key used to enter the BIOS Setup:

1. From the technical documentation to the motherboard

2. From the prompt that appears on the monitor during the POST procedure. For example: if the message "Press DEL to enter Setup" is displayed on the screen, this means that you must use the

Delete key to enter the BIOS. Press the key immediately after the prompt appears on the screen.

Here, as a rule, a prompt is displayed - a key combination with which you can call the utility for flashing the BIOS.

3. Sometimes the prompt on the screen may be missing. Then you need to press the key several times with an interval of about 0.5-1 second after the first image is displayed on the screen.

Attention!!! If there is no manual for the system board, and the prompt does not appear on the monitor, first of all, use the following keys (key combinations) to enter the BIOS:

1. Delete;

2. F1,

3. F2,

4. F3,

5. F10,

6. F11,

7. F12;

8. Ctrl + Shift + S;

9. Ctrl + Alt + S;

10. Ctrl + Alt + Esc;

11. Ctrl + Alt + Del;

12. ESC.

Sometimes (very rarely) other keys can also be found:

1. Ins;

2. Alt;

3. Ctrl;

4. Ctrl + Esc;

5. Ctrl + Alt;

6. Ctrl + Alt + Ins;

7. Ctrl + S;

8. Ctrl + Shift + Esc;

9. Ctrl + Shift + Alt + Del.

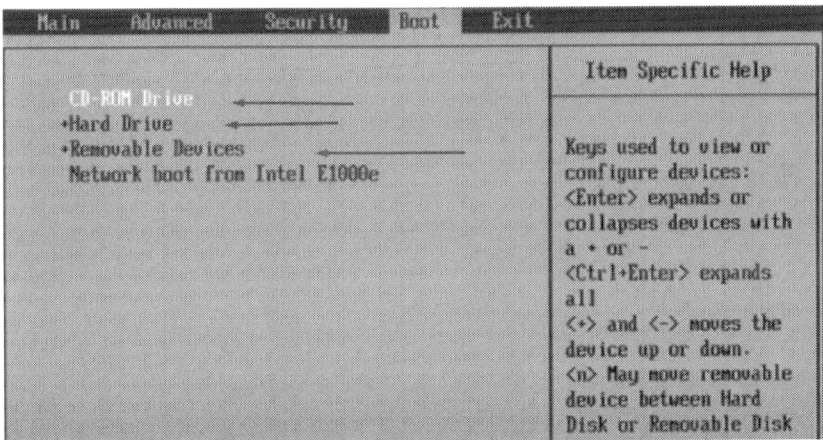

After booting from the installation disc, you will see the language selection menu. As a rule, English will be immediately selected, and you just need to click Next. If you ever installed previous versions of Windows (versions 7 and 8), then this window will seem familiar to you.

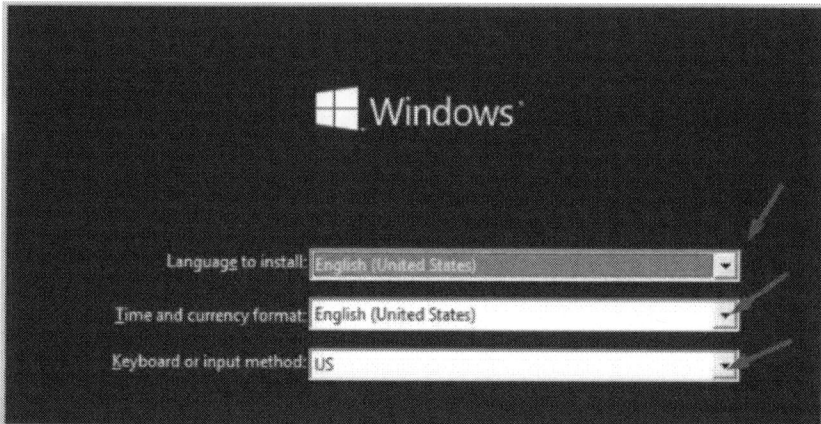

After that, you will see a window with a single Install now button.

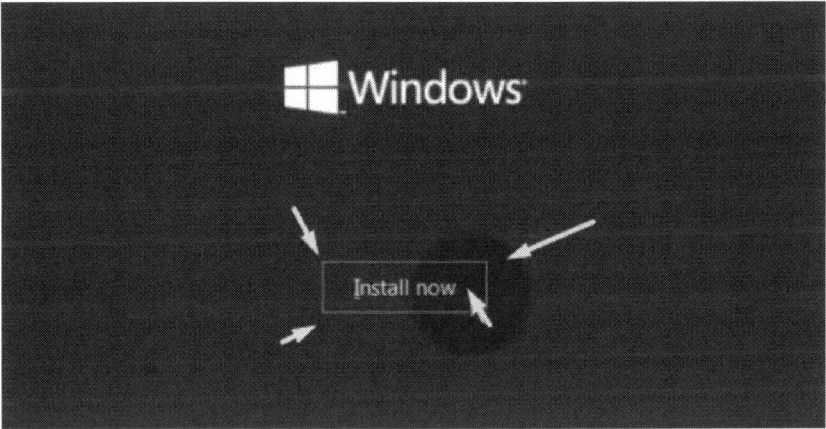

Next, you need to enter the product code

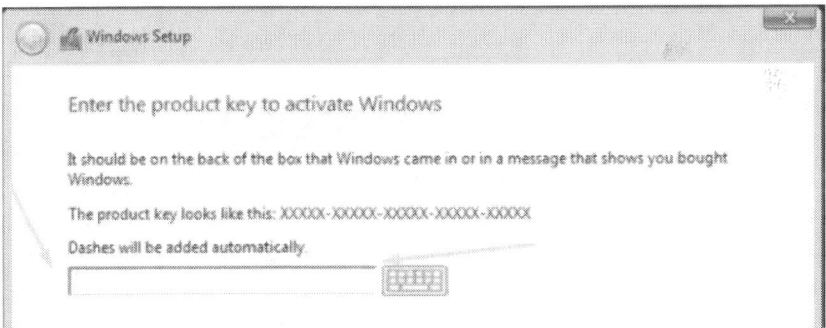

After you accept the terms of the license, you have to choose the type of installation.

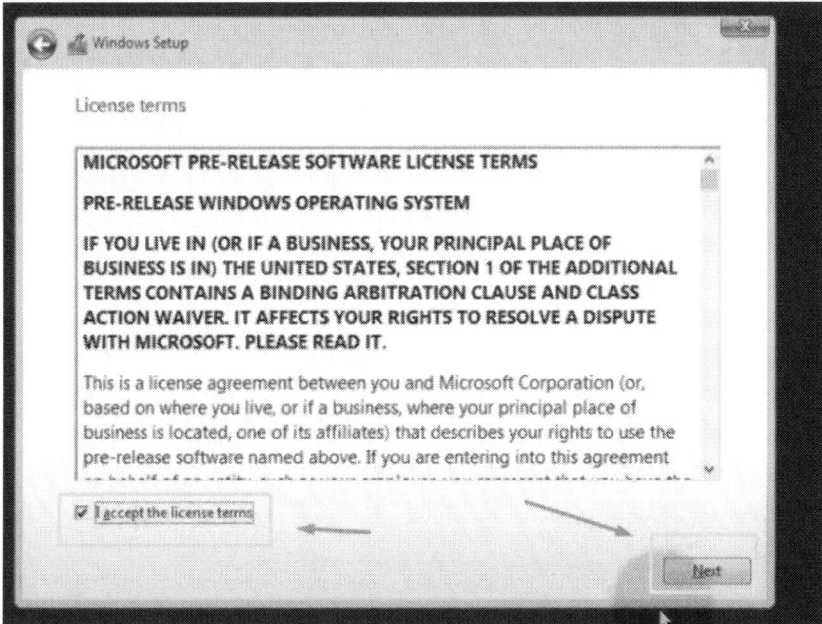

Since we are installing the system on a new computer, you need to select Custom: install Windows only.

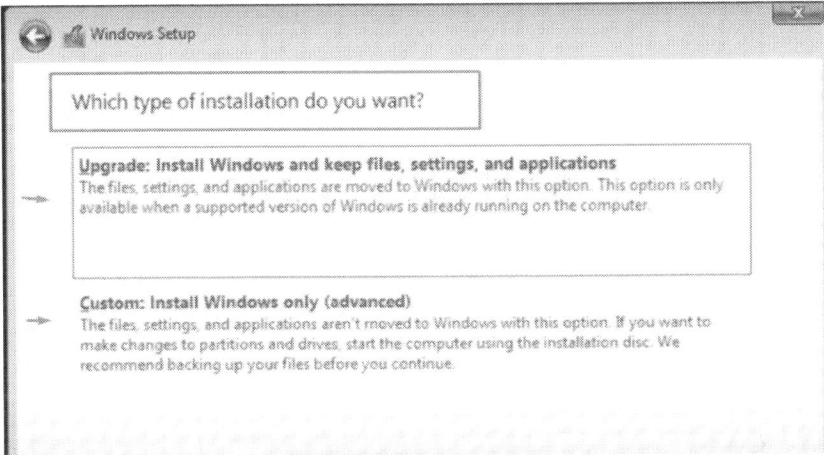

Immediately after that, you need to select the drive on which you install Windows 10.

Attention! For normal operation of Windows 10, your computer must have free disk space. The minimum needed (as Microsoft claims) is 20 GB for the 64-bit version and 16 GB for the 32-bit one. But Microsoft is a bit of a lie. A 64-bit assembly literally in a matter of hours after installation increases its volume to 25 GB. But with 32-bit everything is much more pleasant - it immediately took 6 GB after installation and update. Only 6 GB.

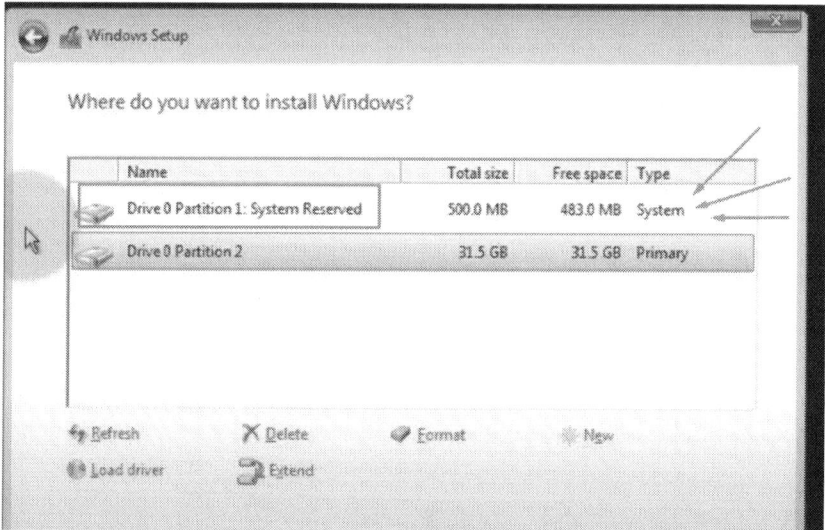

Next, the system installation process should begin. After it is installed automatically, your personal computer will reboot. Depending on the performance of the hard drive, this process can take from several minutes to several tens of minutes. On SSDs, installation takes place in minutes.

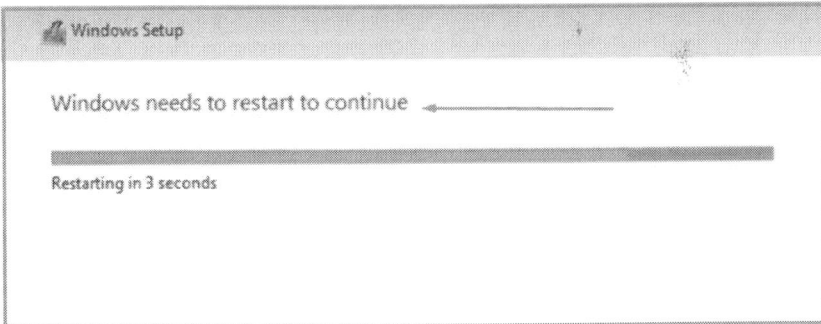

After the reboot (which will be fully automatic), you will see a black screen with the Windows 10 logo and the preparation process.

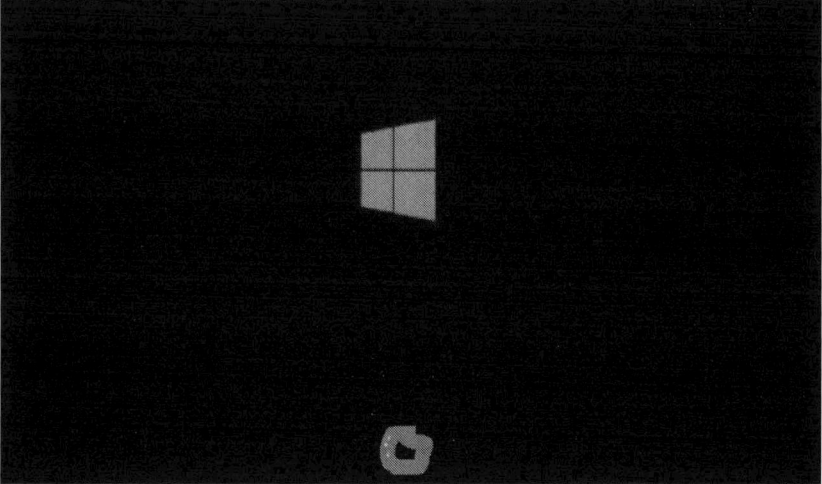

After that, the installer will offer to set some parameters. All the parameters that are proposed to set by clicking the Parameter Settings button, can be changed after installation, so I suggest that you do not waste time installing them now, but just click the Use standard parameters button.

Then, Windows 10 will try to get critical updates from the Microsoft website, but this is only if the computer is immediately connected to the Internet, for example, using a local area network connection (to a provider or router), all other connection types require preliminary configuration.

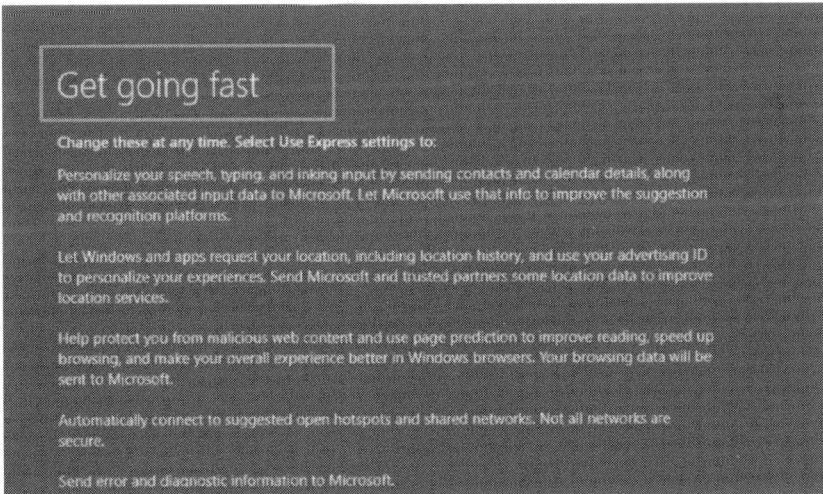

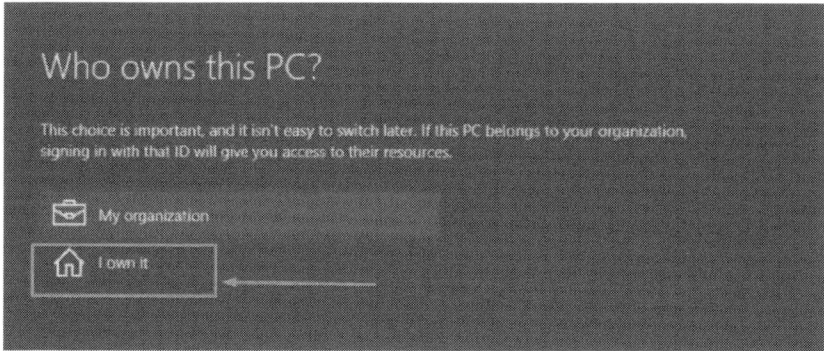

Create your Microsoft account

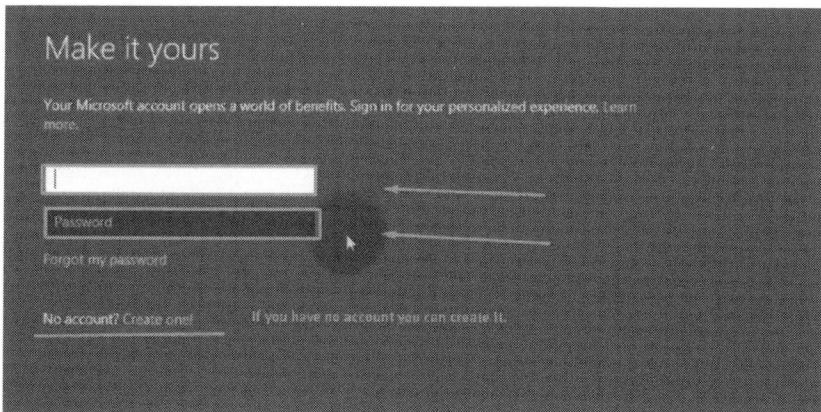

The next step in setting up your personal computer will be to create a user account. If you have an account, you just need to enter the Login & Password. In Windows 10, unlike Windows 8, they do not offer to create a Microsoft account during installation. Later, if you want to use certain functions of the system, you will be asked to create a Microsoft account.

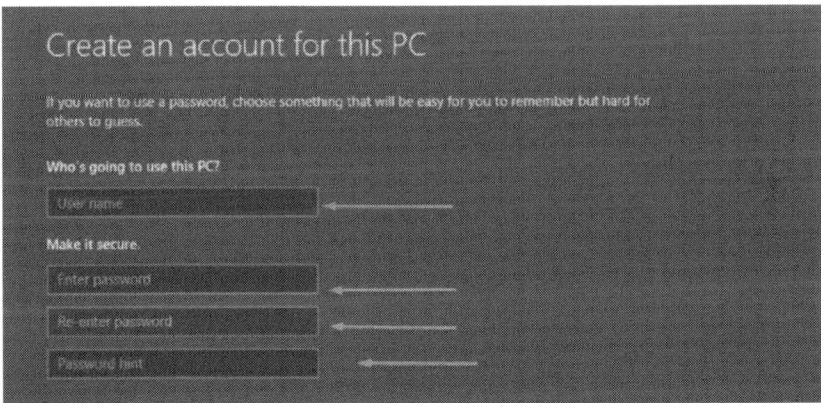

So enter your username and password. You can not specify a password, but for the security of your computer, it is better to do this. Having even the simplest password significantly increases security when encrypting data using standard system tools. Therefore, if you plan to work with data on the computer that you want to encrypt using EFS, be sure to set a password.

After creating a user, the system will offer to wait a bit while it configures applications.

After configuring applications, the system will prompt you to choose whether you want to allow other computers and devices on this network to detect your Personal Computer. If there are other computers in your network, select yes, if there are no other computers and you are not planning to work on the local network, then select No.

Actually, that is all. You will see the desktop of the new version of Windows.

Chapter 2: Start Menu and Settings. Everything a beginner needs to know.

Start Menu

Start Menu Button is located in the lower-left corner of the desktop. With this Button, we will gain access to the programs and applications installed on your computer. In addition, they are presented in the form of icons on the left side of the menu and "glance" on the right.

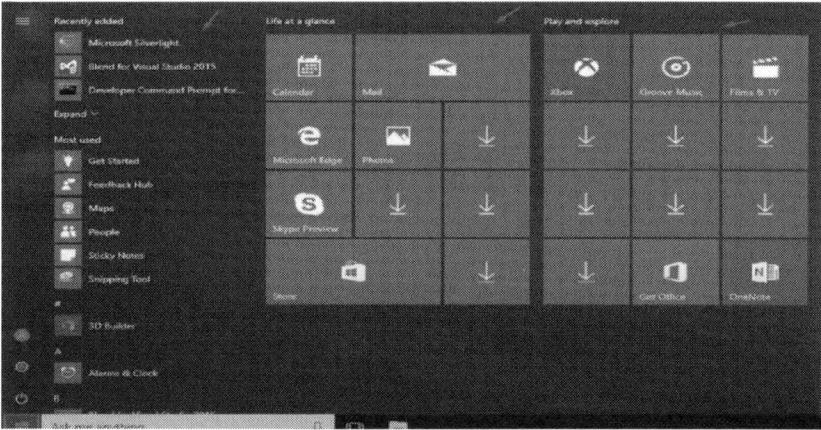

Let us start with the left side: it contains the main buttons already familiar to us. Repeat them:

 - Search-icon.

 - The Shutdown and Reboot menu icon above the Start button.

- The Settings menu above the Reboot icon.

The most used and Recently added icons

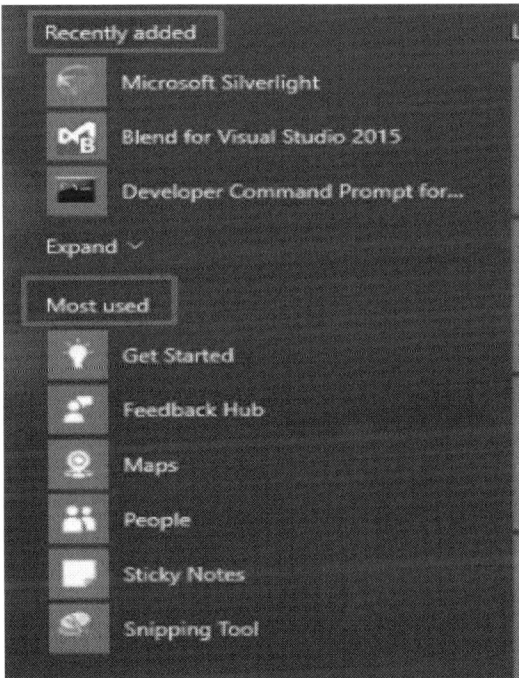

Let us go to the basic information, go to the list of programs and applications - to the icons and tiles.

To make things easier for us, Windows puts at the top of the column a list of Recently Installed and Frequently Used Applications that you work with most often.

We already understand that we can launch any program from this list by clicking the left mouse button or "tap" if we work in tablet mode. In addition, what will happen if you use the right button or "long tap" with your finger?

Here is what: A context menu appears with a list of recent documents opened in this program! In addition, using the same menu we can:

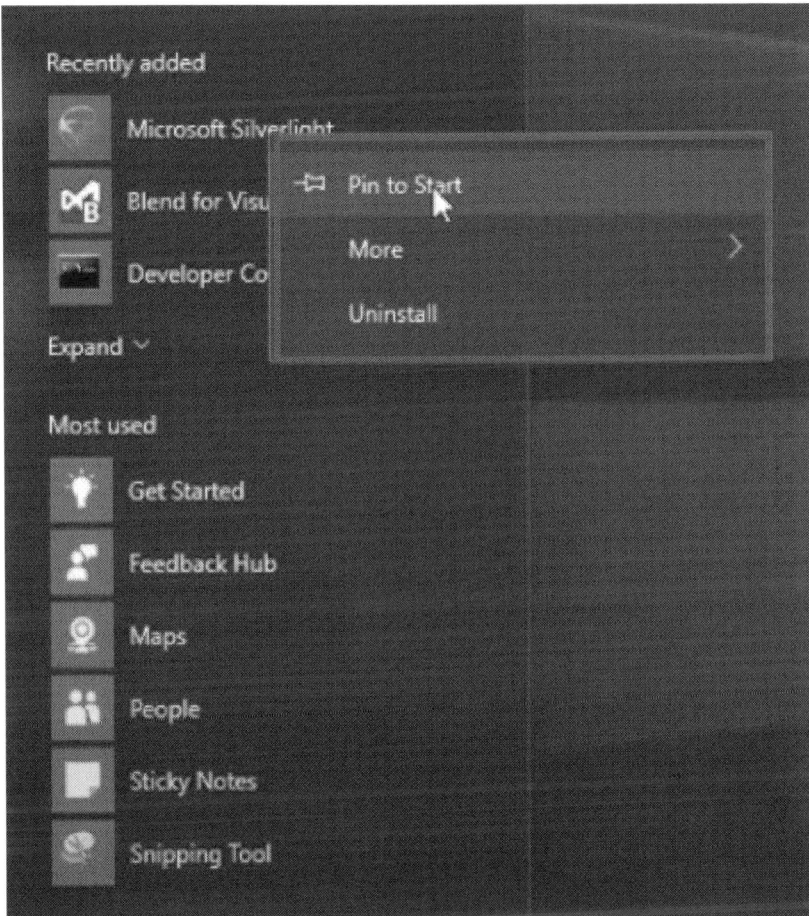

a. Set the program in the frequently used menu (Pin to the home screen).

b. Fix its icon on the taskbar (taskbar) at the bottom of the screen.

c. Uninstall the program from the

computer.

d. Run the program as administrator (we have to do this very rarely - and only with old programs adapted for Windows 7).

e. Open the folder in which this program resides.

This trick works not only with the Frequently Used and Recently Added menus, but also with any icon in this column.

Pay particular attention to the first two points: it is better to place the icons of the applications you need right away on the Taskbar at the bottom of the screen or transfer them to the Desktop. When you do not need to open the start menu each time, you will have to search for a program in a long list much less often.

By the way, we can simply drag the icon of the selected program onto the desktop with the mouse while holding its right button. But even if you haven't done this, you can always quickly find the program you need without the Start menu - just type part of its name in the Search menu at the bottom of the screen.

The list of the apps

Below are located the icons of all the programs installed on the computer, arranged in alphabetical order. How many of them and what a long list there is! Now imagine that you need, say, the Word program, and it is at the end of the list. If you do not want to waste time rewinding the list, simply click (or tap with your finger) the letter at the top of the list and you will see a "table of contents", from which you can quickly jump to any letter.

Start Screen (Tile Panel)

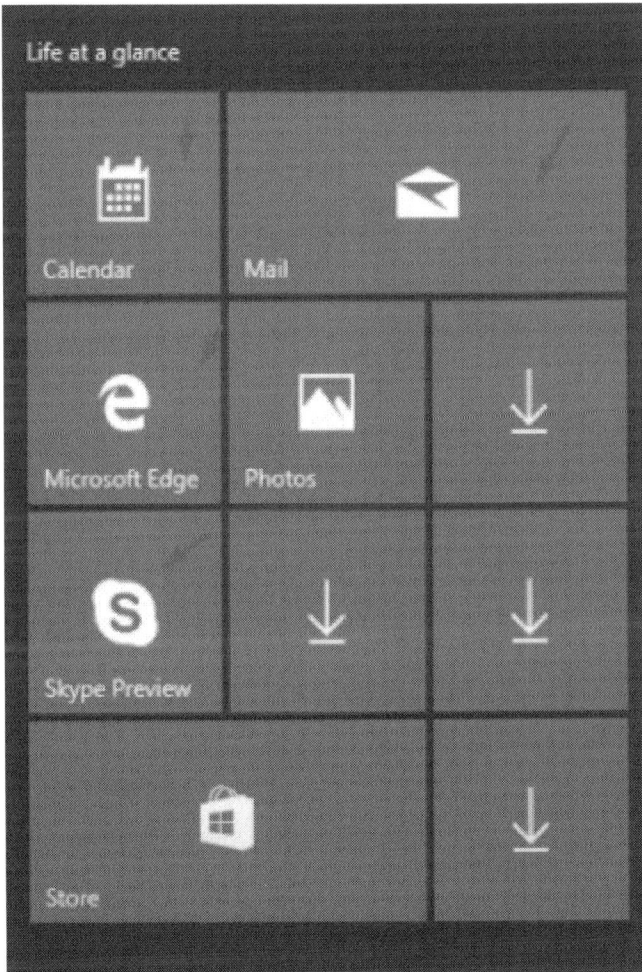

"Tiles" of new universal Windows applications are placed on the right (in Tablet mode, this area is called the Start screen, and it really takes up the entire screen).

"Live tiles" differ from ordinary icons in that they can display various notifications - for example, about new letters from the mail program, current stock prices and currencies, news, etc.

You can drag and drop tiles from place to place, as well as change their size and add them to the Taskbar at the bottom of the screen (for this you need to call the Context menu with a right-click). Unnecessary tiles can be removed (right-click - the Delete command), adding new ones instead - just drag and drop the icons of the necessary programs from the left program panel to the right.

Like the icons on the Desktop, tiles can be combined into Folders - just drag one icon onto another with the mouse.

Windows suggests combining tiles differently by grouping them. Several of these groups - Events and Communication, Entertainment, and Recreation - were already created during the installation of Windows, and in the future, the system will try to "register" tiles into the necessary groups on the subject of applications on their own. But you can create a group yourself by dragging the desired tile with your finger or the mouse (while holding the left button) to the bottom, empty part of the window. And then, by clicking on the blank title, give the new group a name.

You can place the tile of any program from the All Applications menu on the

Start screen - just click its icon with the right mouse button and select the Pin command on the start screen. In the same way, you can send the desired icon to the Taskbar or "taskbar" at the bottom of the screen - usually those applications that we always want to have been given this honor. And also an extra icon that you don't need can be removed from the Home screen (or the Taskbar): the right mouse button is the Detach from the home screen command.

Start Menu Settings

Like any element of the Windows interface, the Start menu can be configured using the Options menu. In this menu, we select Personalization next to Start.

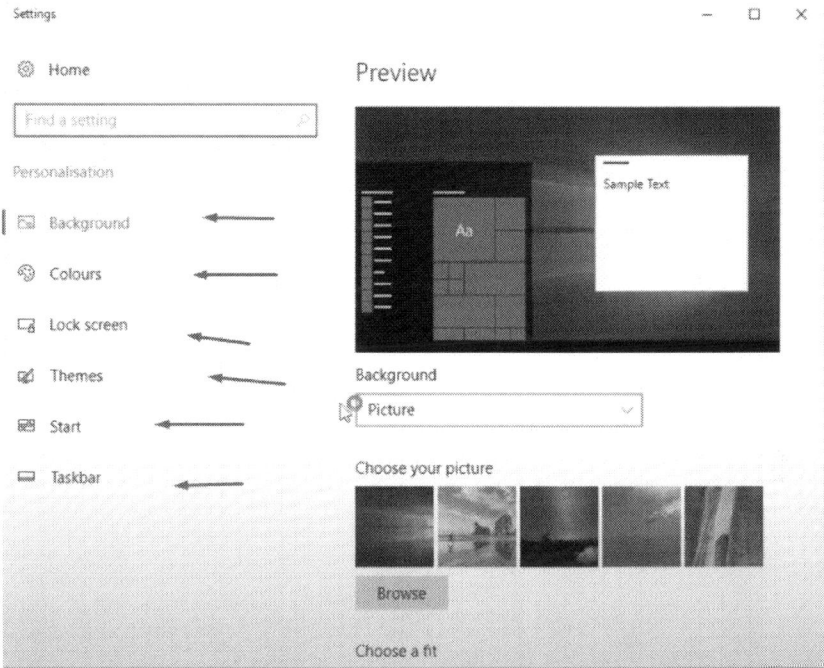

However, there are not many settings here: you can disable the folders of Frequently Used, Recently Installed Applications folders at the top of the menu, as well as the Recommended for Installing Applications panel (this should be done first). In addition, the Start menu settings allow you to open the Home screen in full-screen mode and select the list of folders that will be displayed on the tile panel.

Start the context menu

We are already acquainted with the concept of the Context menu - it appears if you click on the icon not with the left button, but with the mouse button (in tablet mode, it is called up by a long press - "long tap"). We already called it for the icons in the Applications menu ... and what happens if you right-click on the Start button itself.

The context menu of this button stores many useful tools; however, we will need most of them at the more advanced stages of exploring Windows. Therefore, it can be called the "administrator menu".

From here you can quickly call up the Explorer window - the main tool for traveling through the files and folders of our computer, the Shutdown and Parameters menu, the Task Manager (in it you will find all the applications currently running) ... As well as a number of hidden tools necessary for fine-tuning the system - PowerShell Command Prompt, Network Connections, Disk and Power Management, a device manager that collects information about the hardware of our computer. It should be remembered that the fastest way to access most of them is from here (although there are other ways to call each tool).

1. For example, in order to turn off the computer through the Start menu, we need three clicks of the mouse, and

through the Context menu, only two clicks and one movement of the mouse.

2. To access the list of applications we will need to first click on the Start button, then on the Settings button, and then select the Applications menu there. This is done twice as fast through the context menu of the Start button,.

3. The program for Disk Management (you need it to quickly "format" and split hard disks and other media connected to your computer) you cannot find at all, except through the Search and Context menus of the Start button. And rightly so: this tool is dangerous in inexperienced hands.

Settings Menu

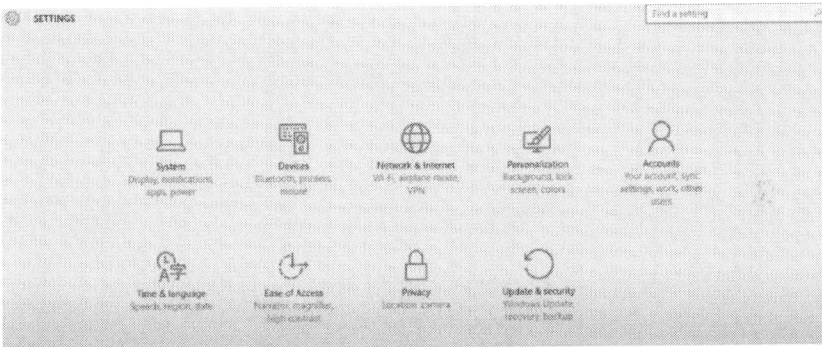

However, the most necessary tools for configuring the system are collected in the new Settings menu - and for the last time remember that to adjust, twist some levers and wheels in the system, we will refer to it. Prior to this, all operations for setting up the computer were carried out through the Control Panel - it was saved in Windows 10, but was pushed into the background, as it is not suitable for the "touch" mode of operation and is too overloaded.

A link to the Options can be found at the top of the Start menu ... However, I recommend immediately pinning the icon directly on the Taskbar at the bottom of the screen: we will have to click on it quite often. How this is done, you already know:

First Step: Open the Options window from the Start menu;

Second Step: then right-click on the gear icon that appears below;

Third Step: select Pin to taskbar.

Search Menu

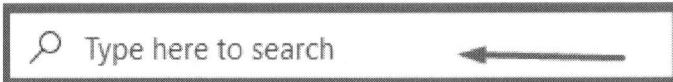

In fact, acquaintance with Windows 10 would be worth starting with the built-in search engine. We will use it constantly - both in "tablet" and in "classic" mode. The Search menu is launched through the icon next to the Start button: thanks to it, you can search both on the Internet and on your computer, (you can search by documents, program names and settings, even for pictures and music).

| All | Apps | Documents | Settings | Photos |

Top apps

| W Word 2013 | Paint 3D |

🔍 Type here to search

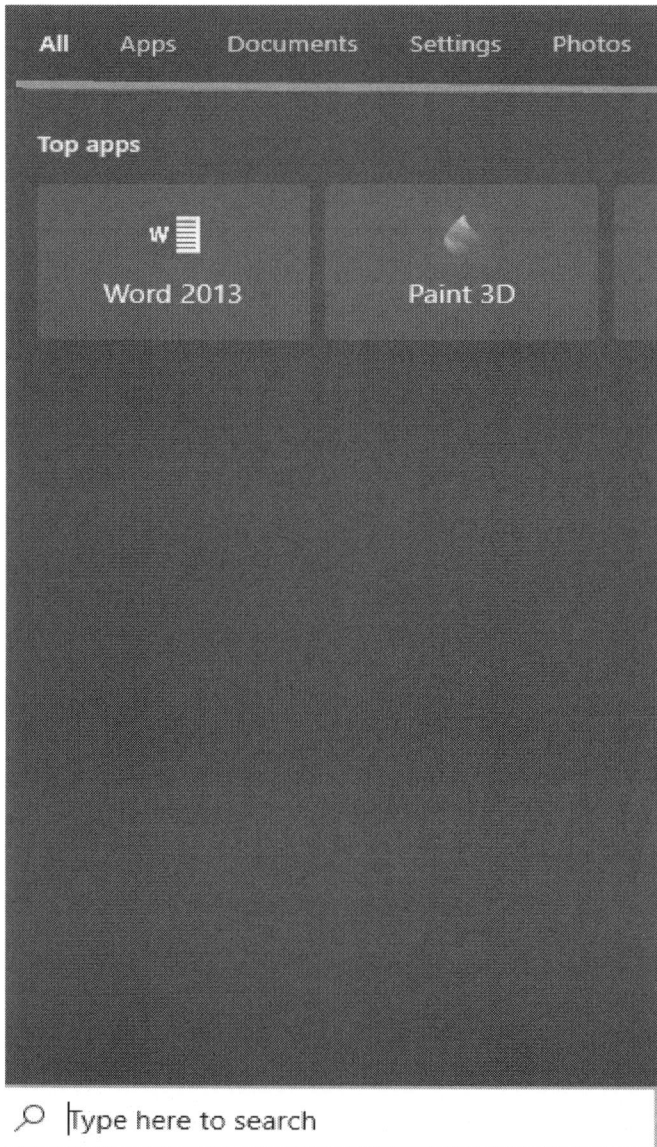

<u>Here is an example for you!</u> For you to get to the Backup Settings in the

Desktop mode, you will first have to right-click in the left corner of the screen, select the Control Panel launch command from the pop-up menu, go to the System and Security section, launch the Support Center, but already there, look for a link to a system recovery tool. Now access to any document, program or configuration tool (there are at least a hundred of them in Windows) is simply obtained through a single Search menu: just type the desired name in the line:

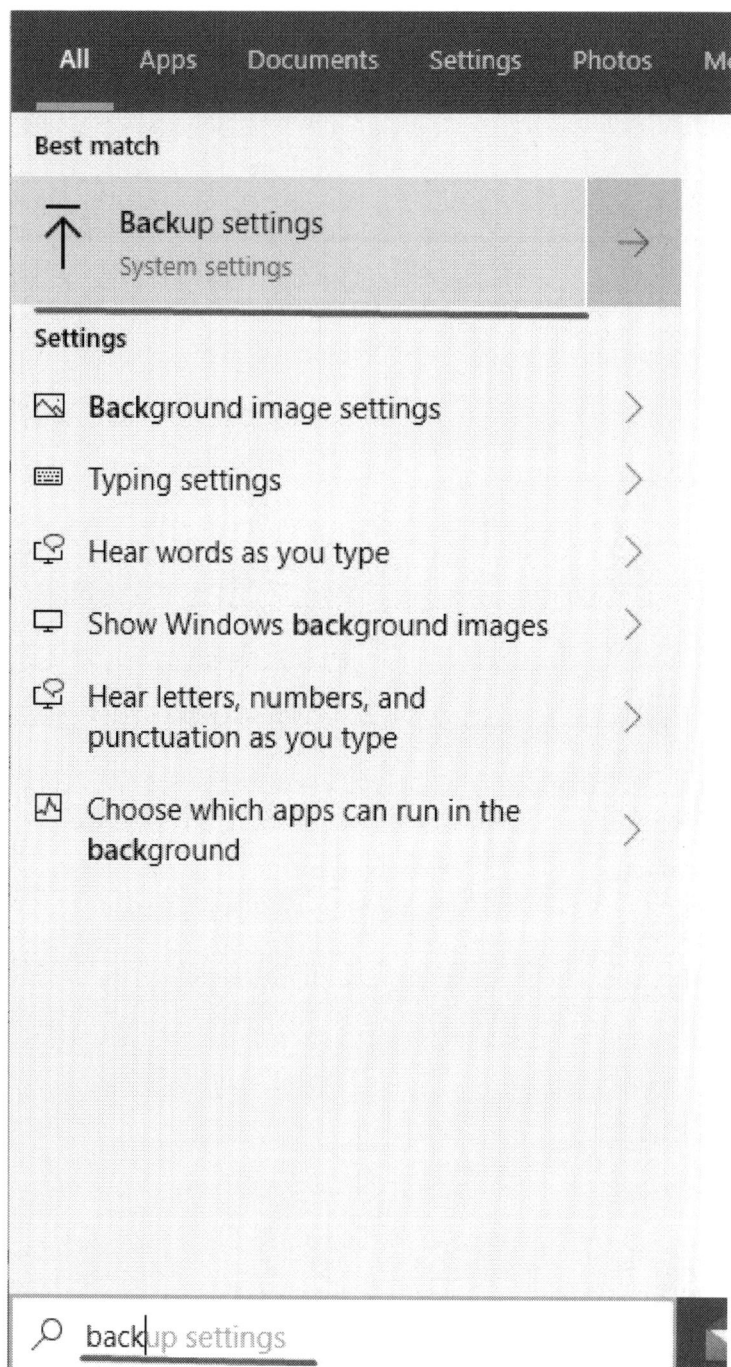

Windows 10

All   Apps   Documents   Settings   Photos   M

Best match

↑ **Backup settings**
System settings   →

Settings

⊠ **Back**ground image settings   ›

⌨ Typing settings   ›

🖳 Hear words as you type   ›

🖵 Show Windows **back**ground images   ›

🖳 Hear letters, numbers, and
punctuation as you type   ›

⊿ Choose which apps can run in the
background   ›

🔎 back up settings

By default, a single list of what is found is displayed in the search results - here are photos, music, documents, system settings and even email. However, you can always sort only the desired results - an additional line with icons below serves for this. Everything is clear here.

Then it will be possible to drag it with the mouse to any part of the Panel, closer to the button and the Search menu.

Toolbars	>	
Search	>	Hidden
Show Task View button		Show search icon
Show People on the taskbar		✓ Show search box
Show Windows Ink Workspace button		
Show touch keyboard button		
Cascade windows		
Show windows stacked		
Show windows side by side		
Show the desktop		
Task Manager		
Lock the taskbar		
⚙ Taskbar settings		

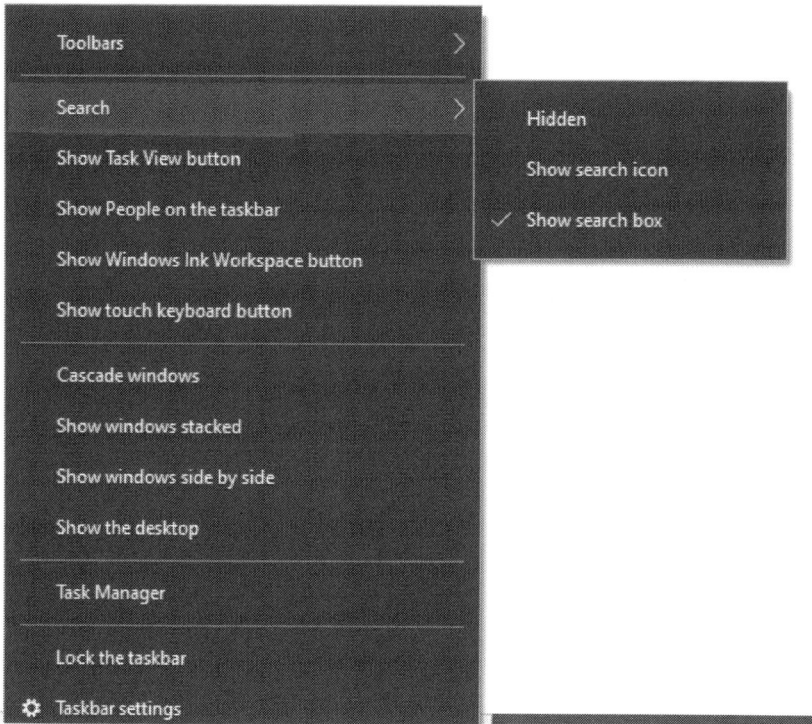

In Windows 10, the search menu is displayed initially as an icon next to the Start button. But you can switch it to the line mode - in my opinion, it is much more convenient. You can switch from one display option to another using the Context menu (right-click, Search next Show search field).

Chapter 3: Classic applications

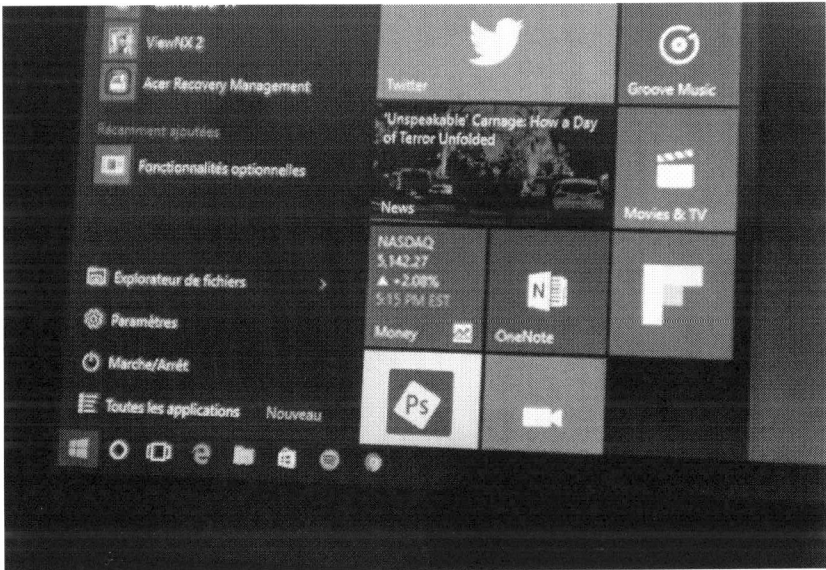

As in Windows 8, in Windows 10 there are both classic applications that are familiar to everyone from previous versions of Windows, and applications of a new format - Metro. The latter are distinguished by a more attractive and modern interface, but in fact, they represent simple applications.

In Windows 10, new applications are launched in windowed mode due to the return of the classic desktop. Many of them have the ability to switch to full-screen mode. Also, the application switches to it when working in tablet mode.

We will not consider classic Windows applications. They are already known to all from previous versions of Windows. You can start standard Windows 10 applications either from the start screen or through the All Applications menu

You can install new applications (if the default ones are not enough for you), you can use the Store application.

Applications:

1. Calendar - the simplest scheduler.

2. Mail is an email client. It is too simple and even many web interfaces of popular services (such as Google) provide more functionality than this client. For serious work with mail, it is better to use another program, for example, Microsoft Outlook.

3. OneNote - an application for creating notes.

4. News - find out what is happening in the world with this app.

5. Weather - the weather forecast for the next few days is now always at hand.

6. Finance - provides various financial information, news from the world of

finance.

7. Xbox - helps you integrate your computer with your Xbox.

8. OneDrive - cloud storage for your files, it will be like an OS for mobile devices, there must be an application for setting an alarm.

9. Calculator - a regular calculator, now in a modern interface.

10. Maps - maps and navigation on your computer.

11. Camera - work with the webcam of your computer.

12. Sports - sports news.

13. 3D Builder - a program that allows you to draw three-dimensional drawings.

All these applications are very simple,

and even a child can figure them out. Therefore, further we will consider only the most interesting applications.

The Calendar

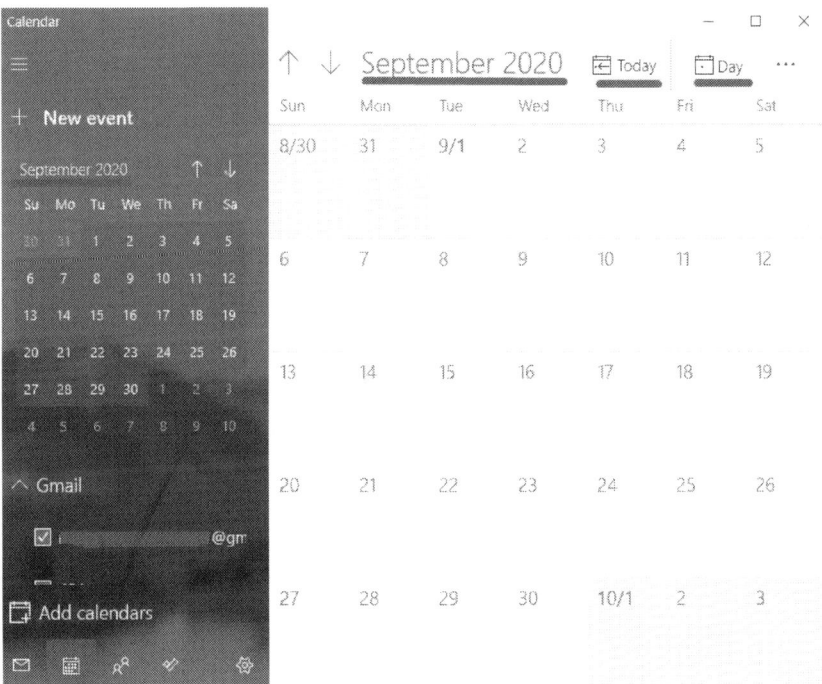

The Calendar application, although simple, can integrate with various calendar services. And this means that if you kept a calendar, say, in your Android Smartphone, the application will be able to connect to the Google service and download your calendar. Of course, all changes will be synchronized, and you can fill out the calendar on your computer (which is more convenient), and view it on your Smartphone when you are far from the PC.

Let's see how to set Calendar to use the calendar from your Android Smartphone. Launch the application and click the Add account button. Record. After that, select the type of account - Google. In the form that appears, enter the email address and password, then grant the application permission to use your Google account by clicking the Allow button.

After that, you can start using the calendar. On the left is the main panel - a calendar for the month, as well as a list of calendars that you work with. As can be seen from fig. 12.7, we have two calendars - one is in the Microsoft account, and the second is in Gmail.

In the upper part of the window, there are buttons for navigating the calendar and changing the viewing mode - Day, Workweek, Week, Today. To add a new event, click the Add Event button in the left pane. Enter the event title, description, time of the event. When adding an event, pay attention to which calendar you are adding it to. The event is currently being added to the Microsoft account.

Click the Save and Close button, after which the event will appear on the calendar.

The Calculator

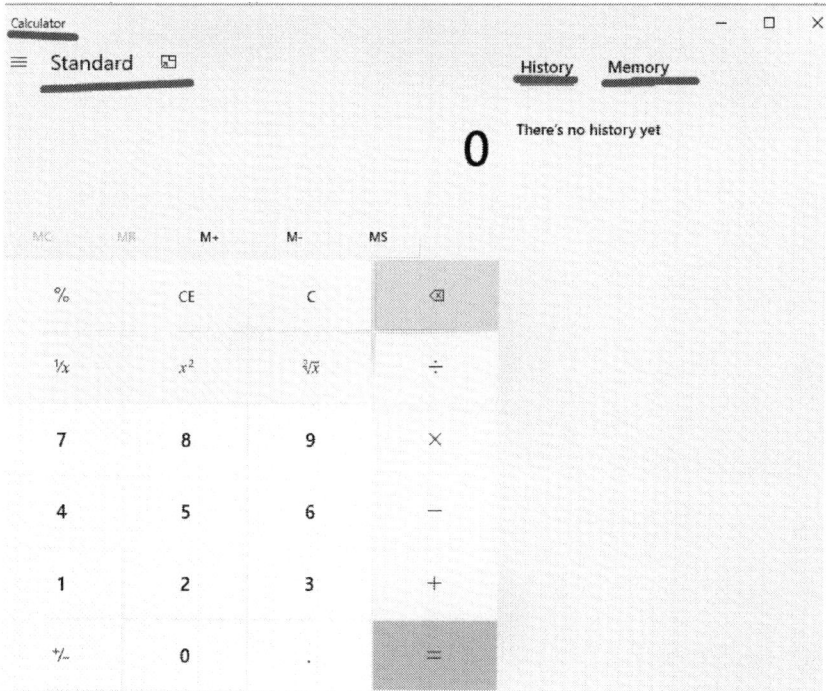

The calculator is a standard application of the Windows 10 operating system, even from the very first released version.

For some, the user is an important feature, the presence of which is of great importance. In the new version of Windows, users often face the problem of launching this application and finding its location.

Windows 10 has many changes, and the location of the calculator is one of them. Once it was in the Start menu in the "Standard" folder, but now it has its own item, among the list of all programs in Start. In some cases, the calculator may not appear at the indicated location. Then try using the search.

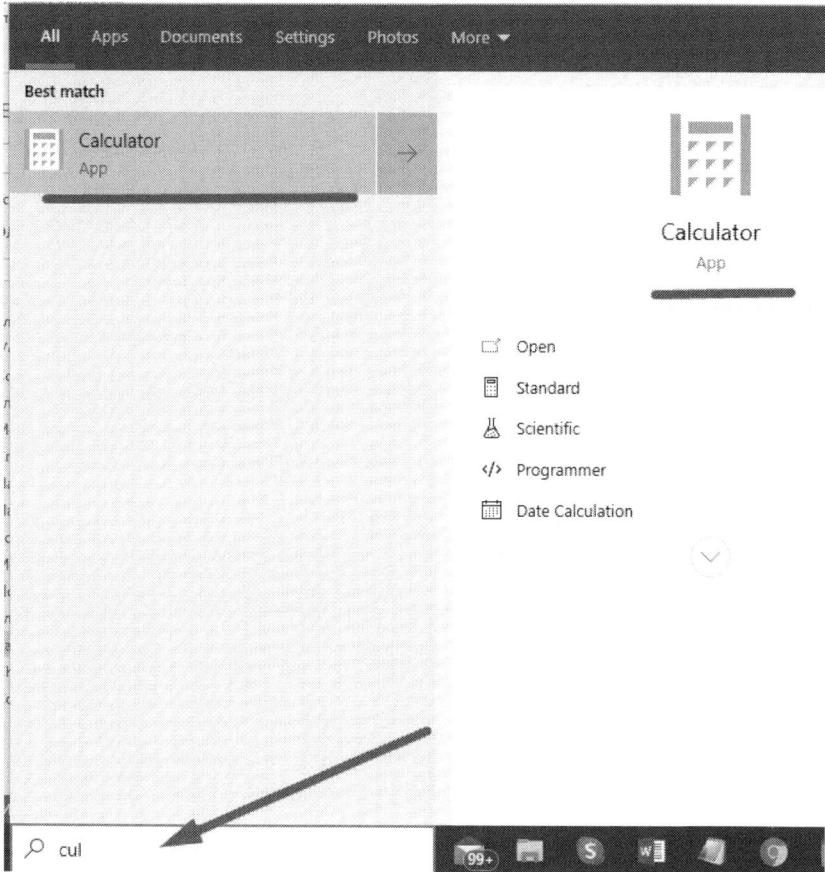

You can still find the calculator if you go along the following path: Local C \ Windows \ System32 \ calc.exe disk. When you find it, it will be more comfortable to create its shortcut and move it to the desktop for more convenient use.

If you checked Start menu and tried to search in the specified folder, and through the search, could not find anything, then most likely your calculator was deleted. There is nothing tragic here, it can be easily installed again. To do this, simply go to the Windows 10 store. In the application search, enter "Calculator" and you will see a list with all existing calculators that you can install on your PC.

In cases where the calculator does not want to turn on, try the following steps:

1) Find the "Applications and Features" section through Start-Settings-System-Applications and Features.

2) Among the programs presented, click on "Calculator". Under the Advanced

Options item, go to them.

3) In the new window, you can see the "Reset" button, and you need to press it and confirm your actions.

After all that has been done, turn on the Calculator application again.

Chapter 4: Microsoft Store

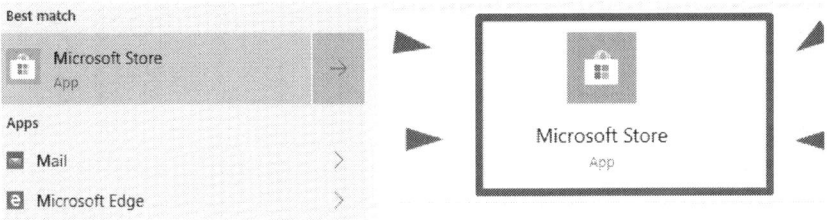

The Microsoft Store is the place where you can buy or get apps for free. You won't scare the modern user with the word "store". We all know that from the similar Google Play and AppStore stores you can download and install applications for free. There are paid applications, but no one forces you to buy and no one imposes paid services.

Back in Windows 8, a separate class of applications appeared - the so-called Metro-applications. Such applications launched in full-screen mode and were adapted for tablets and Smartphones. Such applications are downloaded from the Microsoft Store. In Windows 10, this class of applications runs in windowed mode. From the point of view of the user, there is no difference between the Metro application and the regular window application, unless such applications look more modern. The main difference between regular and Metro applications is that ordinary applications are installed using installers (each application has its own installer) and are uninstalled through the control panel, and Metro applications are installed and uninstalled through the Windows Store.

Advantages of Microsoft Store

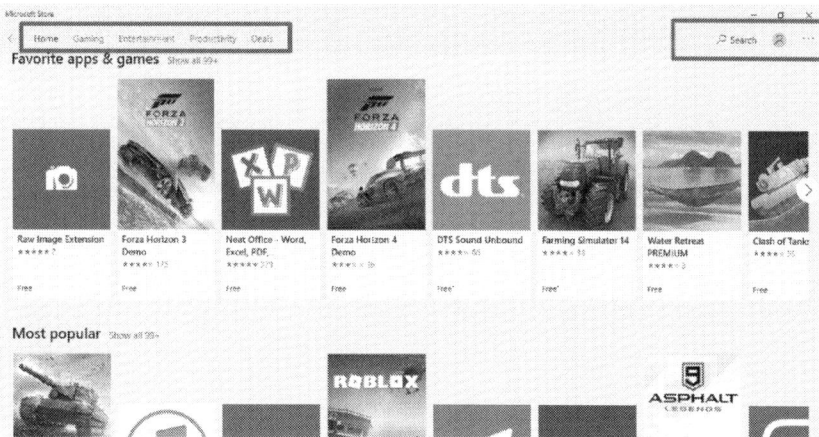

The Microsoft Store has one advantage -
it is tied to your Microsoft account. And
this means that you no longer need to
worry about the distributions of the
program, nor about serial keys, or even
about the list of programs. All this is
stored in your account.

Imagine that you installed several
applications, and then reinstall
Windows. Information about installed
applications will be stored in your
account, and you do not need to
remember what this or that application
was called - just log in to your account.
Naturally, if you bought applications,
then you do not have to buy them again.

Install applications

Launch the Microsoft Store application (in Windows 10, it is simply called the Store). After that, select the application you want to install. It should be noted that if earlier there were frankly few applications and all of them were somehow too simple, now the situation has changed, and in the store, you can find many famous brands of applications that you are familiar with on other operating systems.

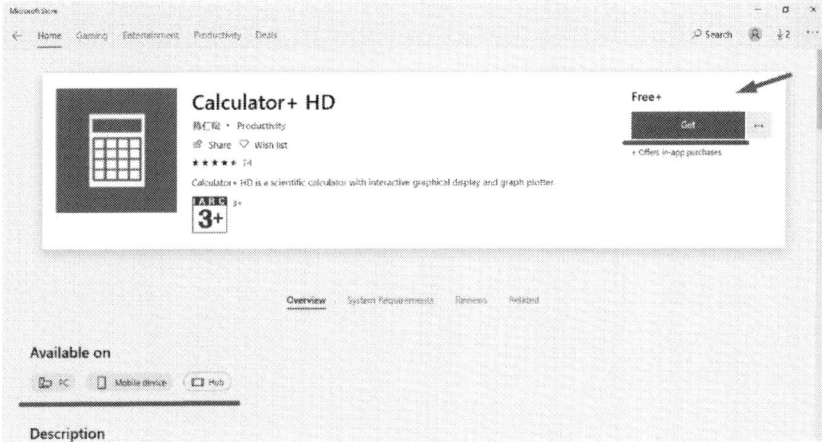

The picture is shown that the application Calculator + HD is selected. To install it, click the Free button. If you are not logged in with a Microsoft account, but as a regular user, then you need to select a Microsoft account, enter the login (email) and password for your account

Further, the Store will show insidiousness and offer to configure Windows to log in with a Microsoft account. select Sign in to this app only.

Actually, that's all. The download and installation of the application will begin. The application download process is displayed in the Store window

At the end of the installation, you will see the corresponding message in the Store window. To open the application, click the Open button or launch it through the main menu.

How to View installed applications

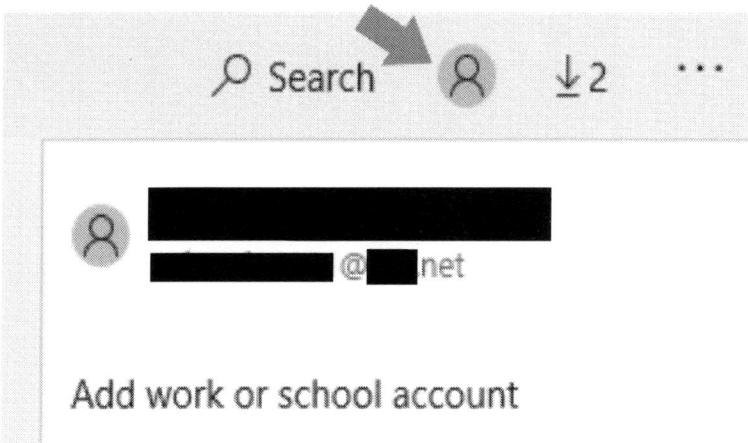

You should Click the account icon and select My Library. You will see a list of installed applications, as well as a list of applications that you previously installed, but which have not yet been installed on your computer.

Applications that were previously

installed (possibly on another computer or before reinstalling Windows), but not installed on this computer, are indicated by a down arrow. You can click this icon to install the application on the current computer.

The application uninstall feature is not provided. Fortunately, they take up very little space. In previous versions, there was a delete function, but in Windows 10, for unknown reasons, it was abandoned.

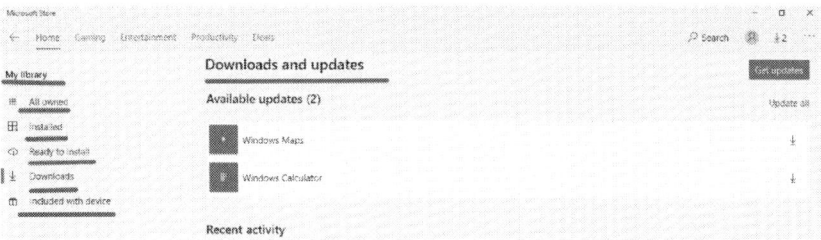

Chapter 5: Taskbar

On the Taskbar, there are icons that are constantly needed.

• Search menu;

• Edge Browser (software for working on the Internet);

• Email programs;

• Microsoft Store, from where we install additional programs.

You can drag the icon of any important program onto the Panel with your mouse, and it will always be accessible.

Or you can do it differently: when you start any application, its icon appears on the Taskbar (temporarily, until the program closes) ... But you can easily leave it there forever: left-click on it and select the Pin program on the taskbar command. See the picture below.

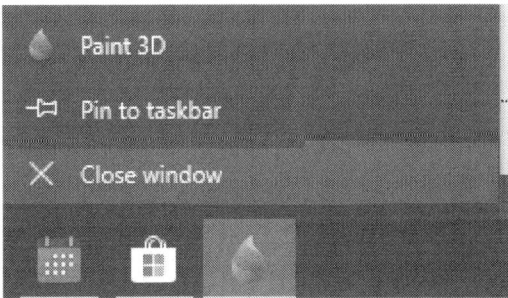

In the same way, you can also remove any icon from the Taskbar (right clicking on the icon is the Remove program from taskbar command). See the picture below.

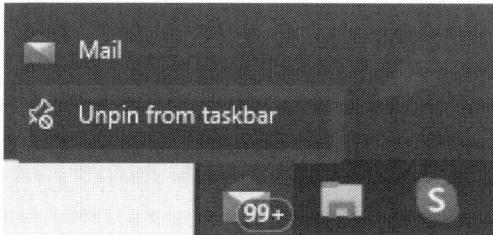

You can manage the windows of already open programs with the help of the taskbar. However, it is worth pointing with the mouse to the program icon in the Taskbar, a miniature image of the program window will appear above it. Alternatively, windows will appear if you have opened several of them. See picture below.

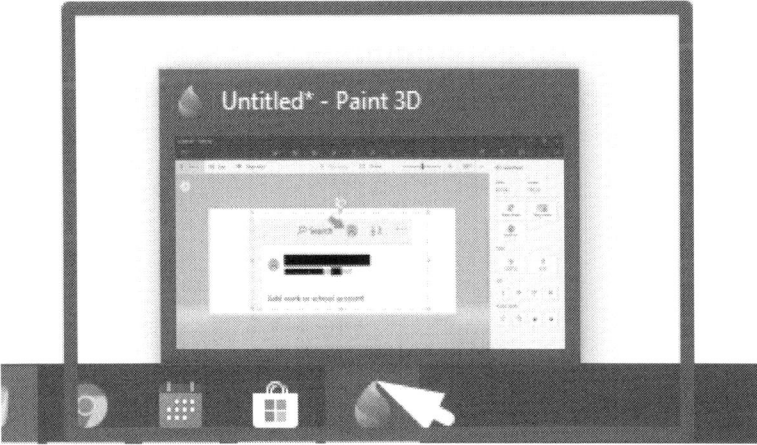

For many programs in the Taskbar, not only thumbnails are available, but also tiny control panels. You can, for example, answer a Skype call, pause a music track ...

If you point to the jumplist with the mouse cursor, all other open windows for a short period of time will become transparent, and the window you select is activated. But only until you move your cursor.

The taskbar settings can be found in the

menu section Settings, System, Taskbar. Here you can also switch the panel to the "auto-hide" mode, attach it both at the bottom and at the top of the screen and change the size of the icons on the taskbar.

Chapter 6: Trey

The Trey in Windows 10 is almost identical to this element of Windows 7, except for a few points. Trey - notification area - a Windows interface tool that is used to display notifications, download programs that work for a long period, display time, and access to some commonly used system functions (network setting, sound settings, battery level of the portable device). Trey is located at the bottom right of the screen.

These icons can be seen in Trey most often:

1. Quick contacts menu

2. OneDrive Cloud Drive

3. Keyboard switch Punto Switcher

4. Connection icon by cable or WiFi

5. Calendar and clock

6. Notification Center

Any icons can be dragged onto the main panel in the same way, by clicking on the already mentioned "arrow". Just keep in mind that you don't need to drag icons from the Desktop to the Notification Panel, it's not for that.

By clicking on the clock on the right, you will open the Calendar, and at the same time get access to the date & time settings, where you can enable additional hours for another time zone (if you need something for some reason). And at the same time set the alarm.

Finally, we remember that clicking the mouse in the lower right corner of Trey frees the Desktop from all open windows, minimizing them into icons on the Taskbar.

As in the case with the Taskbar, additional settings for the Notification

Area can be found in the menu Options, Personalization, Taskbar. In the Notification Area section, you can enable or disable the display in Trey of the icons of any programs claiming to be the "rookery" of this beach.

Notifications

The notification icon in the system Trey is one of the distinguishing features of Windows 10. It opens a completely new tool - the Notification Center.

Windows 10

Your notifications will remain quiet here in Action Center while you're in full screen mode.
Only alarms will break through.
11:29 PM • via Search

| Turn off now | Change focus assist |

✉ **Mail**

Grammarly Insights
Your Weekly Writing Stats + 40% Off Premium
Grammarly Weekly Insights We didn't see any writing activity last wee
Thursday • Gmail

| ⚐ | 🗔 | ✕ |
| Set flag | Archive | Dismiss |

Crello
Logotype catalog test
6/24 • Gmail

Expand   Clear all notifications

| Tablet mode | All settings | Nearby sharing | Airplane mode |

It is here that before your eyes reminders from various programs will periodically pop up - basically, standard applications of Windows itself, such as Mail, clients of various social networks, and Calendar. Notifications about missed calls and messages from your mobile gadget will also be displayed here, including those running Android (I remind you that you need to install Cortana voice assistant on your phone or tablet).

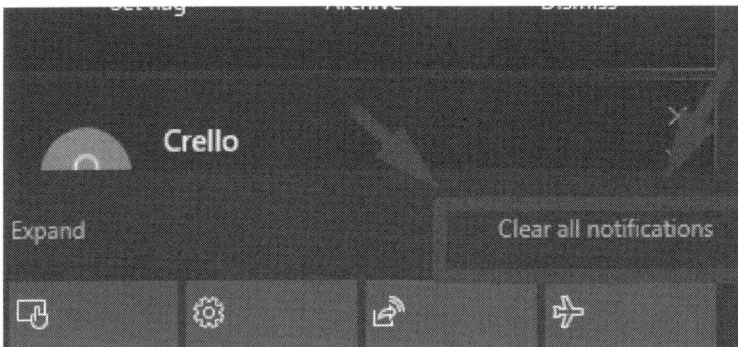

You can clear all notifications at once using the Clear All command in the upper right corner of the panel.

Attention! The most important notifications will pop up right above Trey, in the lower right corner of the screen.

Chapter 7: Desktop

Personalization

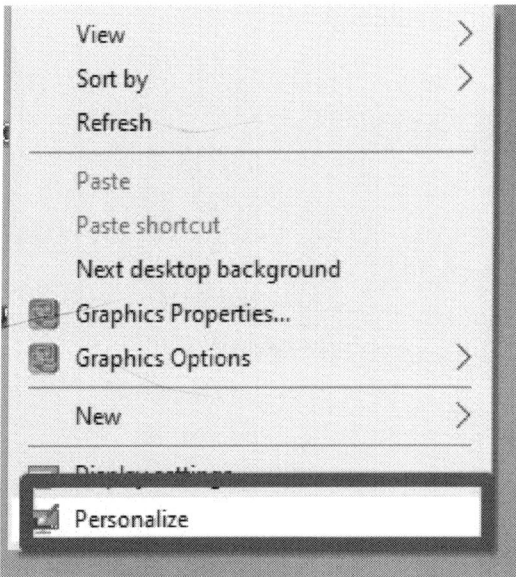

The standard picture that Windows will decorate your Desktop with right after installation is, of course, nice. Windows is easy to customize to suit your own tastes and even mood.

Microsoft calls this "personalization," and all the tools we need are in the Personalization section of the Options menu.

All settings related to Desktop and its design can be found in the menu Options - Personalization.

Let us try to get into it in several ways.

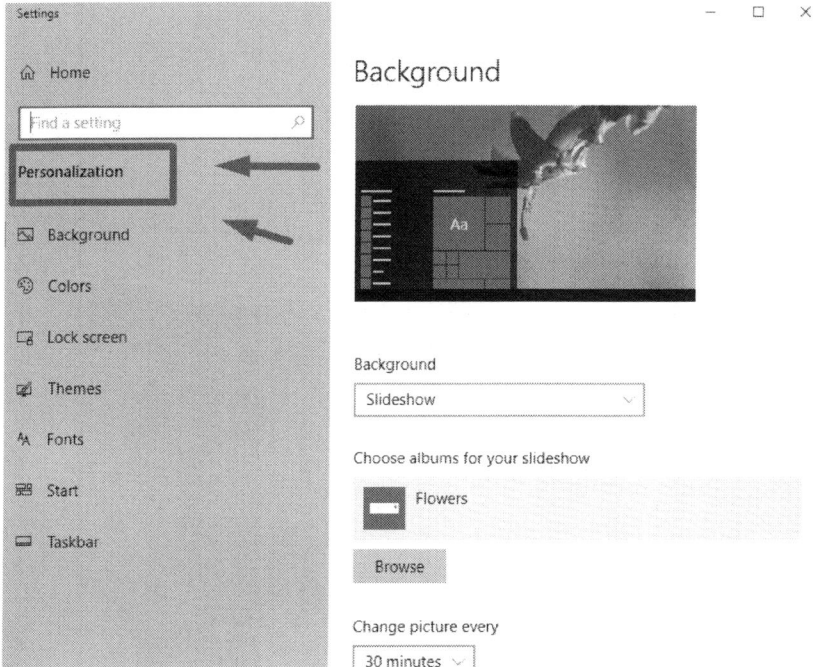

- One we already know - through the Settings icon on the Start menu.

- You can also type the word Personalization in the search bar (in this case, you will be taken to the corresponding section of the old Control Panel - there are a few more settings).

- But the easiest way is to right-click on any available section of the Desktop and select the Personalization command from the context menu.

Here you can replace the background image of the screen, and in the Themes section, you can also see the appearance of the mouse cursor and screen fonts.

Change themes

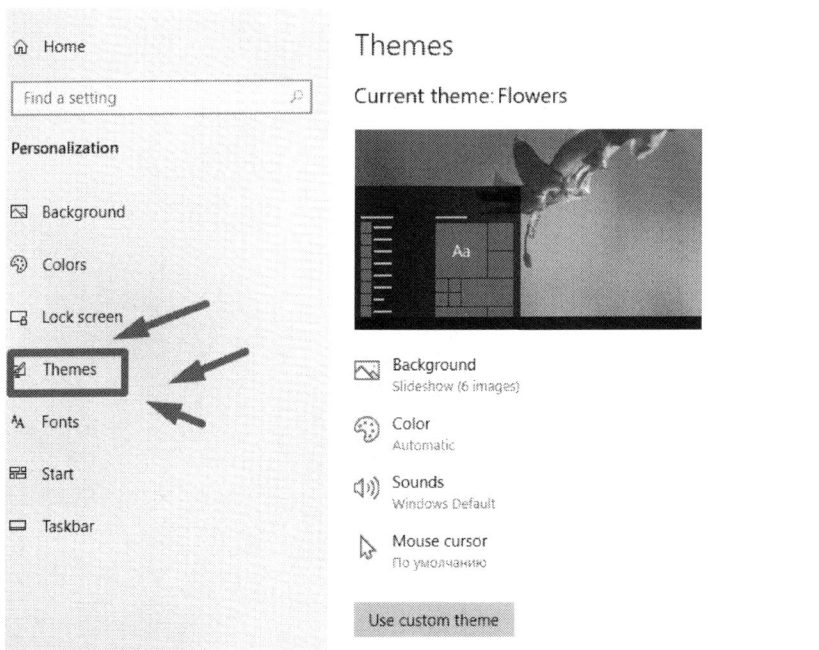

On-screen "themes" allow you to change the appearance and color schemes of all elements of Windows - a background image, mouse cursor and even background sounds. Most topics include several "wallpapers" that replace each other at regular intervals.

A standard set of a dozen topics is, of course, not enough. But you can get new ones for free by downloading them (completely free!) from the Microsoft website by clicking the Other topics link in the Store. There are many beautiful design schemes - with views of the most exotic corners of the planet, photos of deep space, and so on.

Change the picture on the screen

Not all users are ready to experiment with themes - most of them just need to stick some picture on their Desktop. Well, this can be done with the help of the same themes, since a selection of wallpapers is included in each of them.

But if you want to set your own photo as a substrate - no problem!

Right-click on Desktop, go to the Background Personalization menu.

As you can see, we can fill the Desktop with a solid color, without any picture, select a finished photo from the Windows collection or any folder (for example, Images).

By clicking on the Browse button in the Select photo menu, you can set absolutely any picture from any folder as the background - even from the Desktop to which you copied the photo from the Web.

Comment! Any picture can be sent to your Desktop directly from the standard Images folder in Explorer ... Anyway, from any folder: right-click its icon and

select Set Desktop as Background Image

Change the color scheme

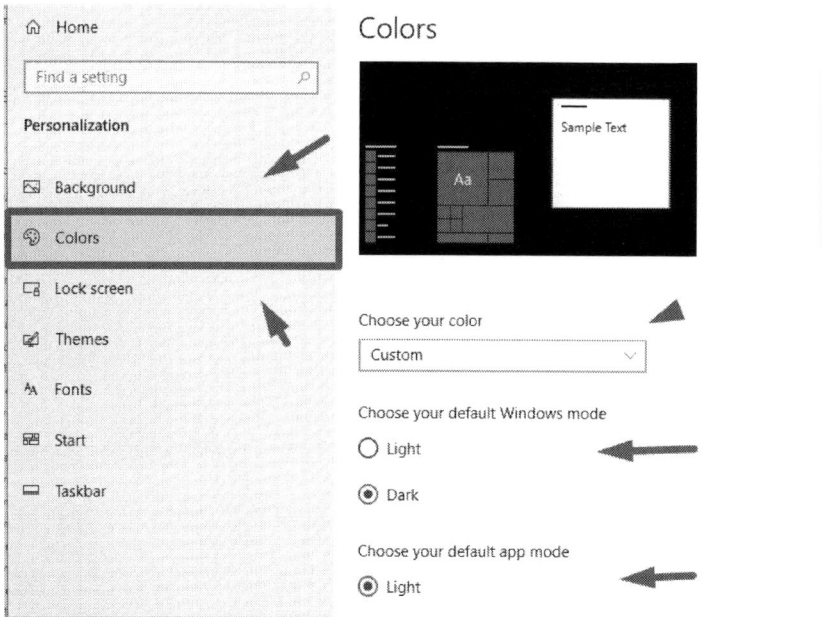

The next menu item Personalization (Colors) is responsible for changing the "color scheme" - fonts, window titles, dice, etc.

Many of us have a favorite color. It is useless to struggle with "color dependence" - it is easier to make Windows "bend under us" and colorize the windows to our taste. And even though the heavenly gamut of Windows is transparently chosen by designers with taste, there are times when they simply "do not lie on your mood". It doesn't matter - by clicking on the Main color selection menu, you can colorize Windows and Windows panels to your taste. Or use the automatic selection of colors, depending on the background image. Also, using this menu, you can choose one of two Windows design templates - Light (it is installed by default) or Dark.

A little lower in the same menu you can enable the display of selected colors in the window titles and the Start menu, as well as enable high contrast settings - this can facilitate the work with Windows for people with low vision.

Font Size, Icons and Screen Resolution

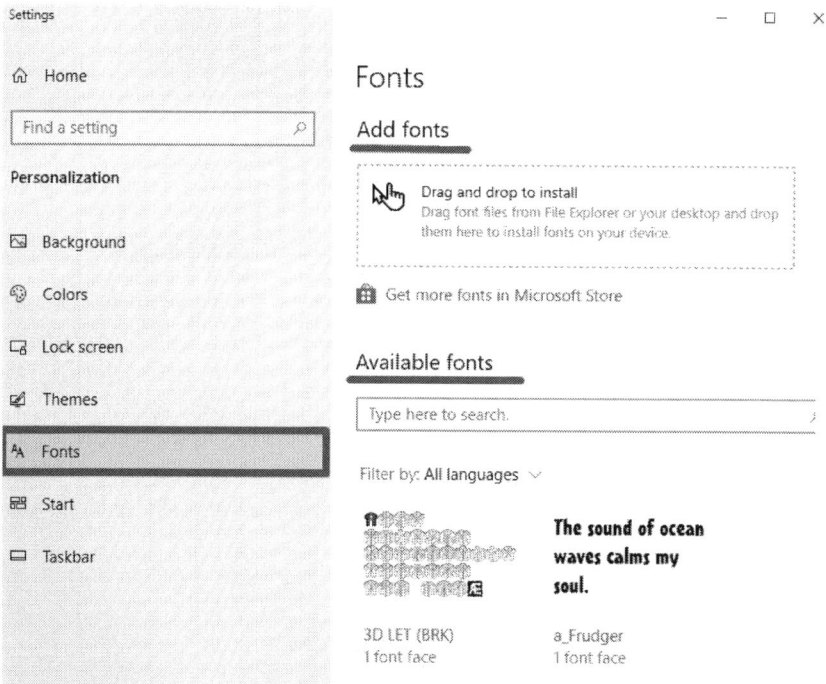

Settings — □ ×

⌂ Home

Find a setting 🔎

Personalization

🖼 Background

🎨 Colors

🔲 Lock screen

🖌 Themes

🗛 **Fonts**

🔳 Start

🖵 Taskbar

Fonts

Add fonts

Drag and drop to install
Drag font files from File Explorer or your desktop and drop them here to install fonts on your device.

🏬 Get more fonts in Microsoft Store

Available fonts

Type here to search.

Filter by: All languages ∨

The sound of ocean waves calms my soul.

3D LET (BRK)
1 font face

a_Frudger
1 font face

Do the small icons and signatures under them annoy you? It is easier to fix them: we again need to call the Context menu of the screen and select the Screen Settings command.

And then, on the Options menu, Resize text, applications, and other elements. The same focus can be done using the System Screen section Resizing text, applications, and other elements.

Here we change the size of all screen elements at once: the icons, the captions under them, and the window titles increase.

Turn on the magnifier

For the convenience of people with impaired vision, the Screen Magnifier program is included in all versions of Windows, with which you can enlarge the image in separate windows (for example, Internet pages in a browser). To find this program is most convenient, as usual, through the button or the Search line at the bottom of the screen (just type the word Loop).

Using the zoom buttons, you can specify the scale of the screen, and pressing the Windows and "+" and Windows and "" keys on the numeric keypad will allow you to quickly zoom in and out.

When working with a touch screen (for example, on a tablet), you can:

• Zoom in and out with a "tap" at the corners of the screen;

• Move around the screen by moving your finger along the border.

You can exit Magnifier mode by clicking on the cross in the upper right corner of the screen.

Virtual Desktops

You can create virtual desktops and switch between them using the View Mode button 'n' on the Taskbar next to the Start button, or using the Windows + N keyboard shortcut.

Attach program windows to any virtual

table (or to all created tables at once) using the context menu command (right-click).

Desktops can also be controlled using hotkey combinations:

Windows + F + D - the new Desktop;

Windows + F + n - delete the current Desktop;

Windows + F + a / c - switch sequentially between Desktops.

Chapter 8: Personal folders

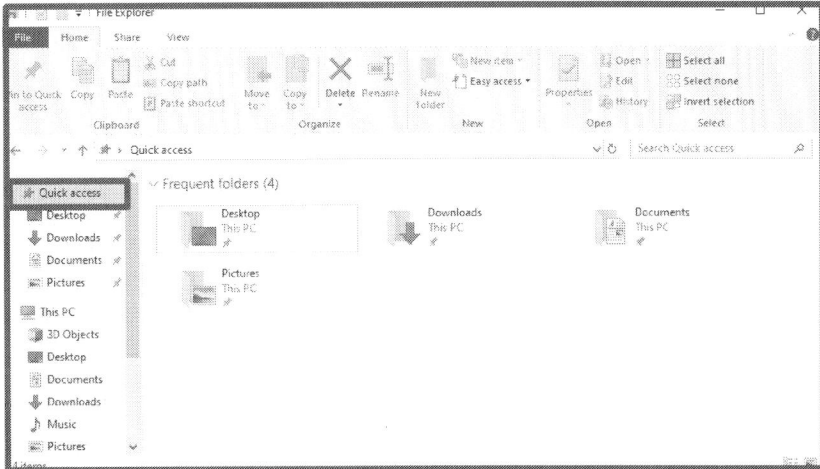

Personal folders

Since we are talking about Personalization, it's time to remember about Personal Folders. All Personal folders can also be found through the Explorer icon on the left side of the Start

menu.

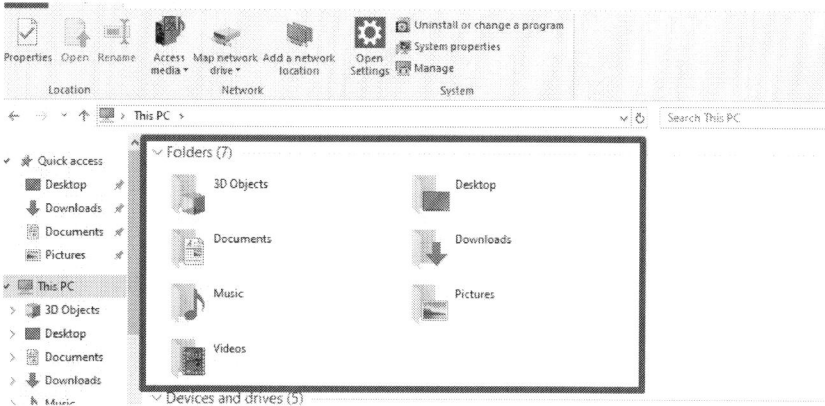

To make it more convenient for both the system and the user - order! So it appeared in Windows Personal folders - Video, Documents, Images, and Music, which we see on the panel.

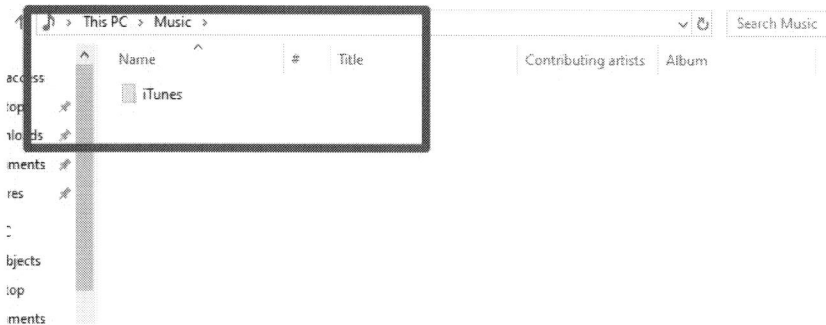

Using Personal Folders gives us some advantages since all Windows services have a special relationship with them. All information in Personal Folders is indexed, that is, any file placed in them can be found through search not only by name but also by content. First of all, this refers to documents that can be found by any keyword or phrase.

All programs are aware of these folders - and if, for example, you copy photos from a smartphone to your computer, Windows itself will suggest putting them in Photos.

Chapter 9: Maintenance, diagnostics and security of your PC

In this chapter, we will look at how to protect your computer from crashes and provide it with complete security.

Windows Update

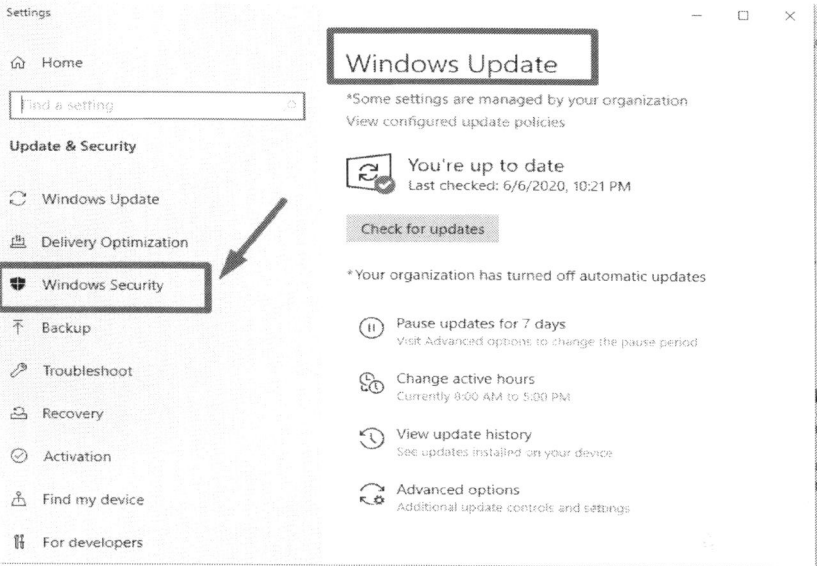

The first and most important security rule: Windows needs to be updated! After all, most of the updates for the system concern security. To do this, you need to go to the Settings menu and select the Updates and Security section.

— □ ×

Windows Update

*Some settings are managed by your organization
View configured update policies

You're up to date
Last checked: 6/6/2020, 10:21 PM

Check for updates

*Your organization has turned off automatic updates

(II) Pause updates for 7 days
Visit Advanced options to change the pause period

Change active hours
Currently 8:00 AM to 5:00 PM

View update history
See updates installed on your device

Advanced options
Additional update controls and settings

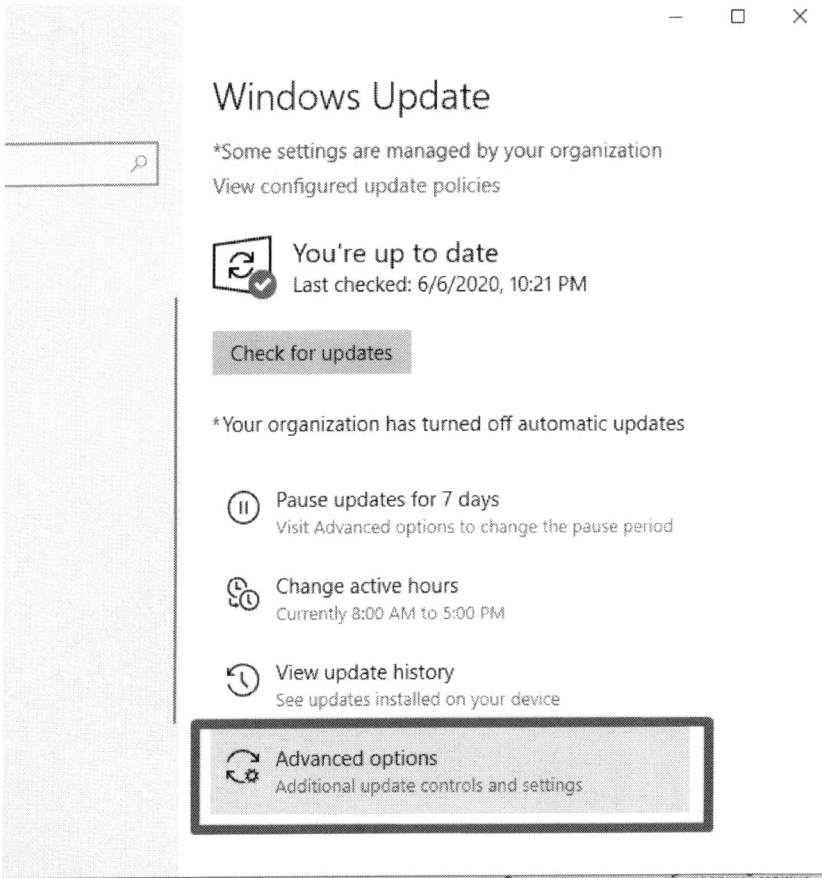

Unlike previous versions, Windows 10 is configured so that you do not need to manually enter the Update Center each time, all this will happen automatically.

⌂ Advanced options

Update options

*Receive updates for other Microsoft products when you update Windows

◉⚪ Off

Download updates over metered connections (extra charges may apply)

◉⚪ Off

Restart this device as soon as possible when a restart is required to install an update. Windows will display a notice before the restart, and the device must be on and plugged in.

◉⚪ Off

Update notifications

Show a notification when your PC requires a restart to finish updating

◉⚪ Off

Pause updates

Temporarily pause updates from being installed on this device for up to 35 days. When you reach the pause limit, your device will need to get new updates before you can pause again.

However, the update mechanism can be customized a little: for this, click on the link Additional options.

Here you can check the box when updating Windows to provide updates for other Microsoft products - in this case, the system will automatically update Office as well. But the most interesting thing is that in this section you can connect to the Windows Insider program, which will give you the opportunity to get new Windows assemblies. And this will give you the opportunity to be among the first to try out new experimental functions of the "windows" - long before they become available to ordinary users of the system. The slider at the bottom of the window will give you the opportunity to choose one of two update schemes: "slow" (only verified updates) and "fast" (all new updates, including ones with functions that are not yet fully debugged).

Windows Defender

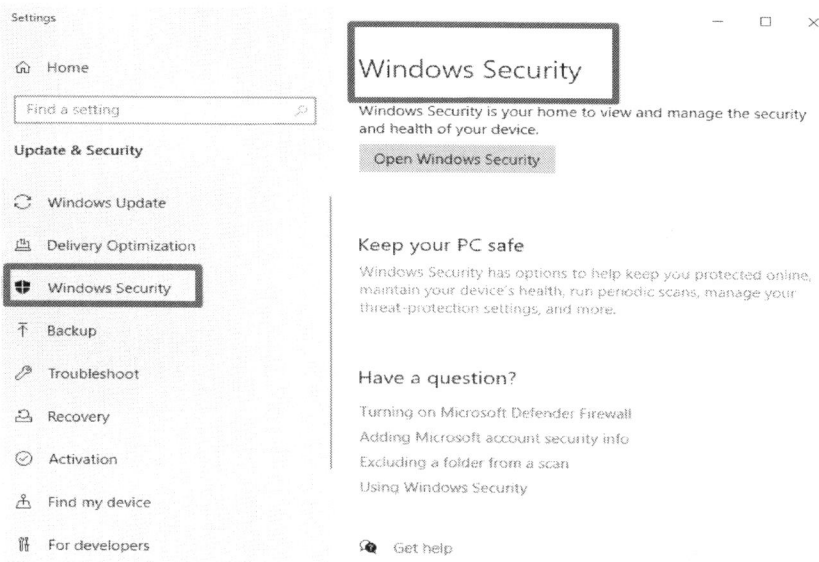

It is a common misconception that any virus, first of all, begins to spoil and destroy information. Or, as a last resort, steals your passwords and credit card numbers from a computer. However, classic viruses are just the tip of the iceberg: today, malware is more subtle:

- Some of them are dug in on your computer in order to attack servers of large companies at some moment together with other infected machines, forming the so-called "botnets".

- Others make changes to the hidden hosts file on your computer, blocking access to social networks and search engines: when you try to reach them, you see a "page not found" message on the screen, or you get to a copy of the original site, but with a proposal to pay for access to it .

- Still others are attacking the browser, every time you launch it, bombarding you with ads and redirecting you to some dubious pages...

- The fourth block Windows itself, displaying the requirement to immediately transfer money to a mobile phone number or Internet wallet. Often, such programs disguise themselves as a warning about the illegality of Windows, and many fall for this bait

- Perhaps the most common blockers in the last few years - this blocks the computer, requiring for the unlock code to send a paid SMS to a specific number or transfer money to an account in the payment system. Other viruses blackmail the user by encrypting all the information on the hard drive. There is less harm from viruses that use the resources of your computer. For example, to "mine" (earn) a virtual currency like Bitcoin: but it really slows down the system

In addition, whether we want it or not, we need a tool to combat all these types of viruses.

Safety and maintenance

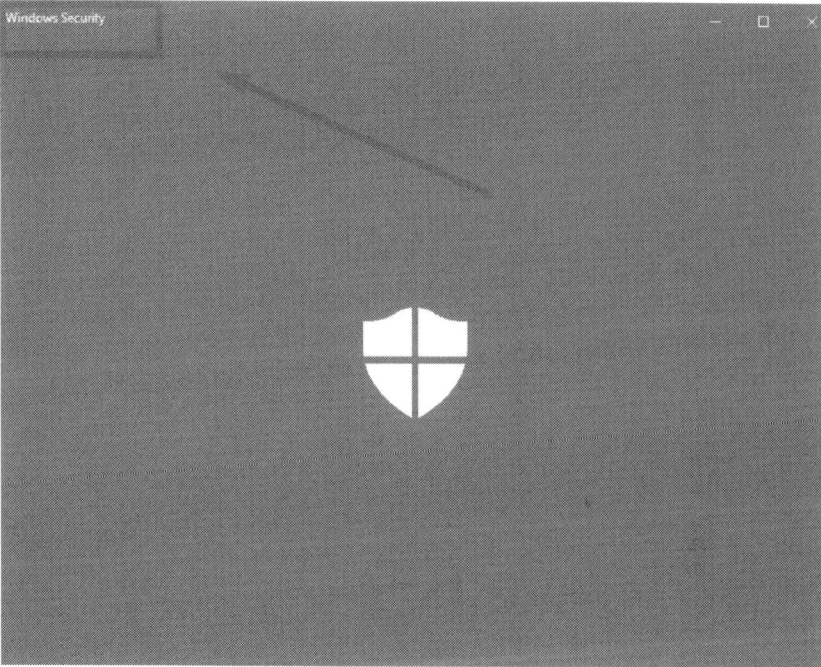

You can get into it in several ways: if there is an icon in the form of a shield in the system tray (in the lower right corner of the screen), right-click on it - and there you will probably find a link to the Center. You can also use the Windows Defender section of the new Settings menu.

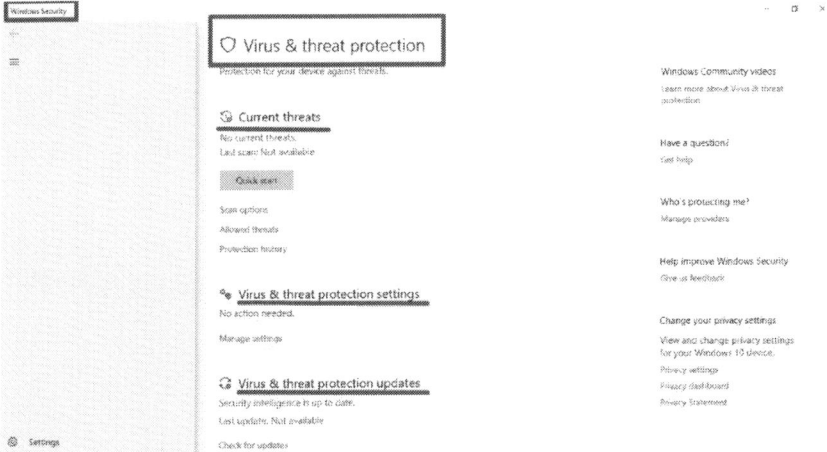

The necessary protection points are already enabled by default, nothing needs to be changed. Although in the updated version of Windows 10 a new tool appeared - Standalone Defender. It is needed in order to remove viruses that cannot be removed when the system is running. If you have doubts about your computer, you can click the Advanced Scan button, then select Windows Standalone Defender Scan for an in-depth virus scan. The check will begin immediately after the computer restarts before the Windows shell takes its place in the operating memory.

In addition to antivirus, the computer is also protected by a system of protection against launching unwanted programs (User Account Control). The principle of its work: as soon as some program on the computer that is not familiar to the system expresses a desire to start, UAC immediately blocks this process and asks you a question, if you yourself understand what kind of program requires allowing it to computer resources, you can enable this action.

UAC is annoying to many to the extreme, so many newcomers

immediately rush to turn it off. In principle, this is not difficult to do ... But is it worth having it - after all, in this case, you are depriving Windows of one of the most powerful security tools. Clicking the button again is easy, but you can be sure that without your permission, no program will be installed on the computer.

If during the installation of the program, this window appears in front of you, and you are ABSOLUTELY sure that the software you downloaded does not pose any danger and the installation should continue, click on the Details link and then complete it anyway.

Chapter 10: Protection against installing unwanted programs and adware

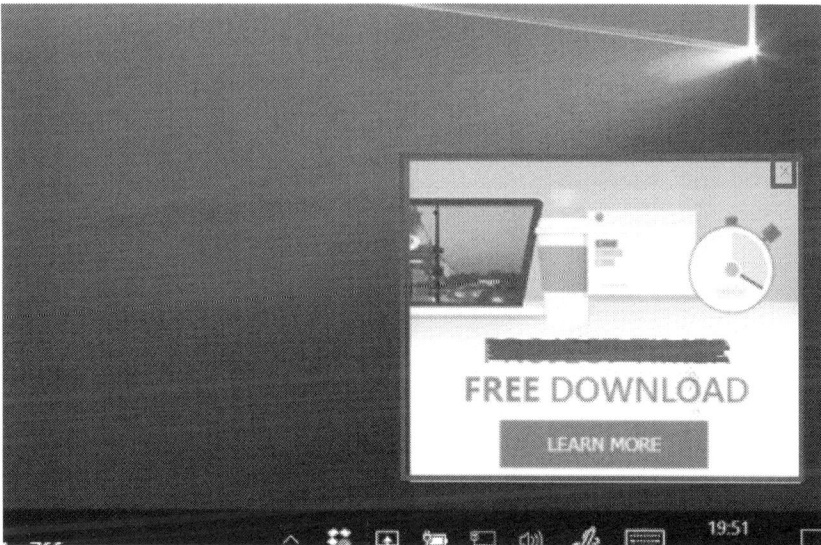

In recent years, classic viruses have become less "aggressive". However, a new misfortune has appeared - advertising!

The tiny Unchecky program (unchecky.com) will help partially protect you from installing unwanted software: after starting it, it automatically removes all the "checkmarks" in the installers of any programs.

However, this method of protection will only work if the developer of the program plays relatively honestly and warns you in advance of the intention to install additional ones. But it happens in another way: a fake "Windows activator" instantly stuffs your system with advertising software, which you won't be able to clean using a standard uninstaller.

Or one rash click on the link in the browser will cause advertising windows to pop up in packs. And the browser will persistently open on the same page with advertising, which can't be changed in the settings anymore - after restarting the browser it will be right there again.

The already installed advertising modules and add-ons for browsers can be handled by these utilities:

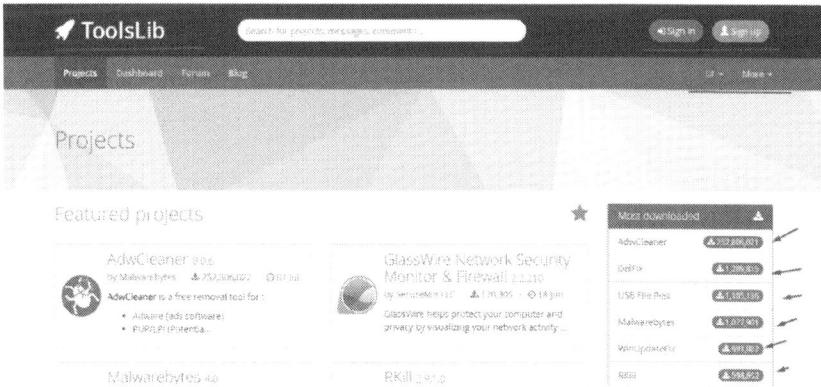

- AdwCleaner — toolslib.net/downloads

- SuperAntiSpyware — superantispyware.com

If this does not help, there is only one way out - to try to "roll back the system" to the previous state of the system using "restore points". And in the most difficult cases, to "reset" the system, losing all installed programs.

Chapter 11: How to Setup a Remote Connection to your Computer

Quick Assist   —   □   ✕

Microsoft Quick Assist enables two people to
share a computer over a remote connection so
that one person can help solve problems on
the other person's computer.

Get assistance

Allow someone you trust to assist you by
taking control of your computer. Please
enter the 6-digit security code that was
provided to you.

Code from assistant

Share screen

Give assistance

Assist another person over a remote
connection.

Assist another person

If you are new to using the operating system, then you may need help. For such cases, Windows 10 has an excellent function to connect to a personal computer via the Network and "fix" problems without getting up from the couch.

Numerous "remote control" programs exist for this case: you can perform almost any actions with it, working with a copy of Desktop, a remote personal computer, as with your own computer.

One of these programs is already built into the updated version of Windows 10 - it is called Quick Help, and you can find it, as usual, through the Search menu.

Now we decide what we will do - to help or, conversely, to ask for help. Let us start with the first option. Click on the button Assist.

The program will generate a six-digit security code for you, which must be sent to your assistant by e-mail or through any communicator. Having received this code, your assistant should start Quick Help, click on the Get Help button and after that enter the code you sent.

After that, your computers will automatically connect, and you can perform any action: transfer any files to the remote computer, etc.

Despite its simplicity, Quick Help is far from the most skillful tool for remote control, it is only good because it does not require any additional software to be installed on the computer.

Chapter 12: Hidden programs

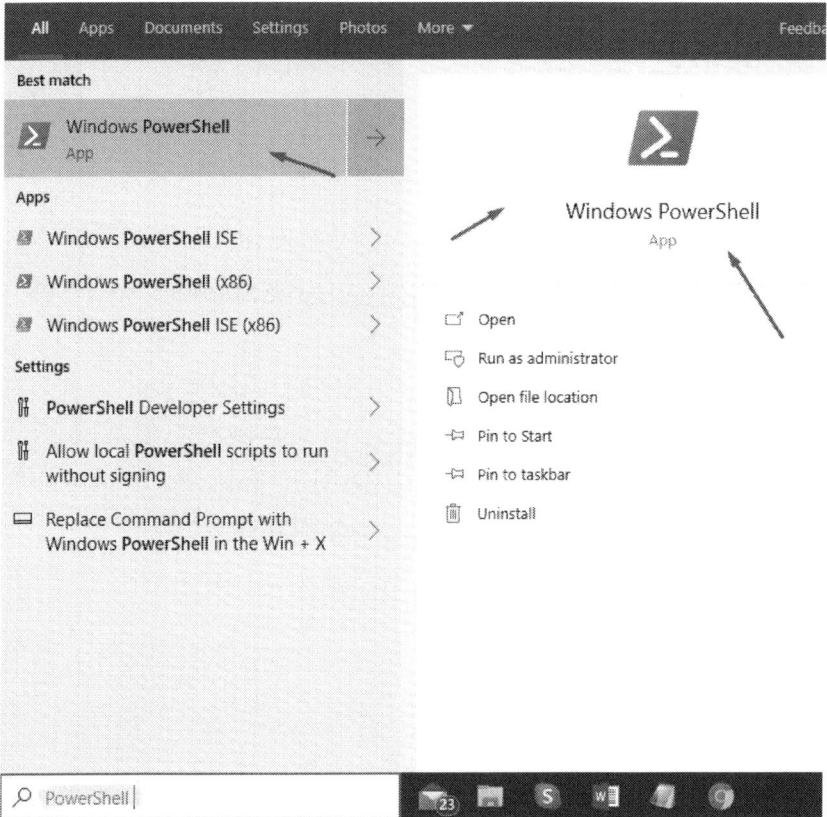

Windows don't want to show some standard programs intended for fine-tuning the computer by default because trusting many of them to the not too skilled hands of beginners is fraught with consequences. Yes, and they are not needed very often . However, getting to the bottom of hidden utilities is not difficult: just type the word Administration in the search line.

The most useful of these tools:

• Disk Cleanup - quickly remove garbage and unnecessary files. I recommend, if you don't replace, then at least supplement this standard program with a separate CCleaner cleaner.

• Defragment and optimize disks. Since Windows scatters data on a disk with the generosity of a sower, most files are fragmented into small fragments and scattered over its entire surface, which, albeit slightly, affects performance. And although defragmentation (that is, collecting disparate fragments into a single whole) today is not as relevant as before, and Windows independently monitors the order, it is recommended to start defragmentation manually every few months. Caution: this does not apply to SSDs!

•System configuration. Fine-grained boot control (don't let your gates climb here without knowing the ford!).

• System Information. A detailed report on the hardware and software of the computer, which can be saved as a text document.

• Memory Checker. Test RAM modules for physical defects and reading errors. Requires restarting the computer.

• Computer control. Perhaps the most

powerful and subtle tool to configure the system, from which many other hidden programs (Device Manager, Services, Logs, etc.) are also available. However, the most necessary (and dangerous) component here is Disk Management. With it, we can quickly clean and format any drive (except for CD or DVD, of course), create and manage disk partitions, and we remember that we can make several logical partitions from a physical hard disk by "breaking" it into partitions.

Attention! To carry out these operations, at least at first, is only necessary with completely new disks that just have been connected to the computer, because most operations involve the complete and final destruction of all data.

• Services. Managing Windows Services,

Windows 10

that is, constantly running system processes. At one time, it was fashionable to "optimize" a computer by turning off some "Unnecessary" services (for example, Fax, support for touch screens, and sometimes even the System Restore service).

In Windows, the "command line" can be called by typing the name PowerShell in the search bar or through the context menu of the Start button, where there are two links to this line at once: normal start and Run in Administrator mode.

134

But those programs that can be called from the command line mode or from the Run menu:

- appwiz.cpl - Removing programs;

- calc - Calculator;

- charmap - Character table;

- chkdsk - A utility for checking disks;

- cleanmgr - Utility for cleaning disks;

- cmd - Command line;

- compmgmt.msc - Computer Management;

- control - control panel;

- control admintools - Administration;

- control desktop - Screen Settings / Personalization;

- control folders - Folder properties;

- control fonts - Fonts;

- control keyboard - Keyboard properties;

- control mouse - Mouse properties;

- control printers - Devices and printers;

- control schedtasks - Task Scheduler;

- desk.cpl - Screen resolution;

- devmgmt.msc - Device Manager;

- dfrgui - Disk Defragmenter;

- diskmgmt.msc - Disk Management;

- dxdiag - DirectX Diagnostic Tools;

- eventvwr.msc - View events;

- explorer - Windows Explorer;

- firefox - Firefox browser;

- firewall.cpl - Windows Firewall;

- iexplore - Internet Explorer browser;

- inetcpl.cpl - Internet Explorer browser properties;

- logoff - Log out of the Windows user account;

- magnify - Magnifier (magnifying glass);

- main.cpl - Mouse Properties;

- migwiz - Windows Transfer Tool;

- mmsys.cpl - Sound settings;

- mrt - malware removal tool;

- msconfig - system configuration;

- msinfo32 - System Information;

- mspaint - Graphic Paint editor;

- ncpa.cpl - Network connections;

- notepad - Notepad;

- osk - On-screen keyboard;

- perfmon - System Monitor;

- powercfg.cpl - Power supply;

- prs - a tool for recording problems reproduction;

- regedit - Registry Editor;

- rrr - Quick launch of Reg Organizer;

- shutdown - Shutdown Windows;

- sysdm.cpl - System Properties;

- syskey - Protection of the database of Windows accounts;

- askmgr - Task Manager;

- timedate.cpl - Setting the date and time;

- utilman - Accessibility Center;

- verifier - Manager for checking drivers;

- wab - Windows Address Book;

- winver - Windows version;

- wmplayer - Windows Media Player;

- write - Wordpad Editor;

- wscui.cpl - Support Center.

Conclusion

Our book was created for both beginner PC users and those who want to learn more about the innovations of Windows 10. We shared with you the latest information - from the basics to professional chips that allow you to dig around deeply in the system.

Printed in Great Britain
by Amazon